W9-CMP-970

ENGLISH COSTUME
FROM THE
FOURTEENTH
THROUGH THE
NINETEENTH CENTURY

Separate Volumes

ENGLISH COSTUME
OF THE LATER MIDDLE AGES
by IRIS BROOKE

ENGLISH COSTUME
IN THE AGE OF ELIZABETH
THE 16th CENTURY by IRIS BROOKE

ENGLISH COSTUME
OF THE SEVENTEETH CENTURY
by IRIS BROOKE

ENGLISH COSTUME
OF THE EIGHTEENTH CENTURY
by IRIS BROOKE and JAMES LAVER

ENGLISH COSTUME
OF THE NINETEENTH CENTURY
by IRIS BROOKE and JAMES LAVER

Also

ENGLISH COSTUME
OF THE EARLY MIDDLE AGES
THE 10th TO THE 13th CENTURIES
by IRIS BROOKE

ENGLISH CHILDREN'S COSTUME
SINCE 1775 by IRIS BROOKE
Introduction by JAMES LAVER

English Costume from the Fourteenth through the Nineteenth Century

Drawn by

Iris Brooke

Described by

Iris Brooke and James Laver

New York

The Macmillan Company

1937

PRINTED IN THE UNITED STATES OF AMERICA

English Costume of the Later Middle Ages

The Fourteenth and Fifteenth Centuries

FOREWORD

AS in the previous books in this series, my aim has been to select interesting and popular garments, head-dresses, footwear, and details of costume of the period. It is not easy in the limited space available to depict the progress of costume during two centuries, and inevitably there are omissions. A great deal of time and thought, however, has been expended on a selection of drawings which will give a maximum of information to the student with limited hours at his disposal and only a slight knowledge of costume.

If the costume of a period is, as Mr. James Laver suggests, the mirror of the soul, there are several interesting reflections in the costume of the fourteenth and fifteenth centuries. The contrast between the dress of the noble and that of the labourer is more striking than at any later period in English history, and it indicates the distinction which the feudal system demanded between the powerful baron and the powerless serf. With the gradual decay of this system later in the fourteenth century, class distinction in dress began a slow process of disintegration which ended only in recent times. Changes in costume were few in the early years of the century, but with the achievement of national unity—the complete fusion of the Norman conquerors and the Anglo-Saxon conquered, and the progress of national freedom in the increasing powers of Parliament—English life showed fresh strength and vigour, which is reflected to a remarkable extent in the costume of the latter half of the fourteenth century. Clothes assumed a new importance, and new and exaggerated fashions made great headway. It was with the arrival of Anne of Bohemia in the 'eighties that the most fantastic and exaggerated fashions made their appearance, and from this time onwards until the Puritan influence of the seventeenth century, costume became more and more ornate. The exaggeration of each phase of fashion beyond the point of absurdity seems to have been the aim of every would-be " Elligant " of the fifteenth century.

The new virility and gladness of English life which found utterance in the verse of Chaucer and his *Tales of the Canterbury Pilgrim* seem to have died with him, but in the century which followed, in spite of the wars with France and the Wars of the Roses, the gay progress of costume continued, and both men and women found ample opportunity for self-expression in dress. Costumes were still fantastic and exaggerated when the acquisition of wealth and material prosperity under the Tudors permitted still further elaboration, so that the fifteenth century closes and the age of Elizabeth opens with pageantry more lavish than at any other period in the history of English costume.

I. B.

1300

1300—1325

CLOTHES worn during the first quarter of the fourteenth century were a motley of a dozen countries. It was a time when England sought and found inspiration for costumes, manners, and furnishings from the Continent and from the East.

It is impossible at this early date to talk of fashion, as we understand the word. Cloth was both expensive and enduring, and one well-woven garment might serve three generations, its usefulness not diminishing with age. Elementary ideas of personal and domestic cleanliness prevailed, and there was a constant struggle against famine and disease. The wars with Scotland and France, and the strife between the Crown and the Barony, left little time for the consideration of dress apart from its utility.

This tendency to severe utility is well illustrated by the two costumes in the frontispiece. These simple loosely-fitting garments, almost devoid of ornament, are typical of thousands that might have been seen in the early years of the fourteenth century.

There is so little change in clothes, and so little variety, in the early period of this century, that one page of sketches is almost enough to show the foundation of practically every type of garment. A man of nobility and wealth wore furs and velvets, and his gowns were usually voluminous and all-enveloping. The women wore a tight-fitting garment, which we will call a kirtle to distinguish it from the outer gown, and over it a surcoat. This garment was split at the sides, and, being sleeveless, displayed the sleeves of the undergarment. A girdle or belt, with pouch attached, was worn either at the waist or a little lower, but little attention was paid to finishing touches. Aprons were worn to a great extent by the people; with this exception, the costume illustrated might be that of a lady of quality. The jester at this time was an important personage in every large household. Later in the century his traditional dress became much more elaborate.

1300—1325 (*continued*)

The coif, a close-fitting bonnet tied under the chin, which enclosed the hair and ears, was worn extensively by men; over this the hat or bonnet was worn. The heads of both men and women inclined to drapery rather than to any formality in headdress. Men wore their hair long—almost to the shoulders. Women always parted their hair in the centre, and wore it in plaits doubled over the ears or confined in a chignon or net. The nets were often ornamented with beads or gilt spangles. In some contemporary drawings the hair is shown in a loose plait or twist hanging down the back.

As the hood, with its gorget and liripipe, became the foundation for dozens of head-arrangements throughout the fourteenth century and the first half of the fifteenth century, it is perhaps advisable, at this stage, to explain how this fantastic fashion began. At first the hood was merely a cowl with a point at the back, with a gorget hanging down over the shoulders. In the next stage the point at the back of the hood was elongated, often to an absurd length, by the addition of a long pipe of the material, or a " liripipe," as it was called. The lengthening of this appendage and the ornamentation of the edge of the gorget were seized on with delight and elaborated to ridiculous extremes by the dandies of the period.

In the early years of the fourteenth century the opening in the hood, which had been previously left for the face, was placed on the head, and the gorget then fell like a scarf from the side or the top of the head, on to one shoulder, and the liripipe on to the other. Later, the liripipe was wound round the head, and the gorget with its jagged edges stood out like a cockscomb. The front part of the facial opening was rolled back to form a brim, and during the fifteenth century this was stiffened, and the liripipe became a wide scarf which was often draped round the chin. The slow evolution of headgear from a simple cowl to the absurdly fantastic head-dresses of the fifteenth century can be traced with ease in the following pages.

1325—1350

THE two costumes illustrated here, of about 1340, have assumed a definite cut and shape which previously had been lacking in both men's and women's attire. The figure-fitting garments are much more attractive than the somewhat shapeless clothes that had been prevalent during the early Middle Ages. The clinging lines were often achieved at this time by lacing down the back, from the neck to the waist.

The working-classes were still wearing the less restricting garments, tied loosely at the waist with a leather girdle, instead of the ornate and wonderfully jewelled belts worn by the wealthy.

The two figures here represented have been taken from the tombs erected to the memory of two of Edward III's children, both of whom died in infancy. That of the boy shows us one of the very few examples of men's civil attire, as obviously the little boy was too young to be represented in armour. The elaborately dagged cloak, with its square enamelled buttons, the high collar, the golden circlet, and pointed bejewelled shoes, all show an advanced stage in fashions for this date, although it is, of course, possible that the tomb was not erected until several years after the deaths of the children.

The golden net on the head of the little princess is interesting as an early example of the emphasis of ornament in front of the ears. The long clinging lines of her cotehardie and the tight-buttoned sleeves are the earliest examples of a fashion which was to last a century or more.

1325—1350 (*continued*)

Few indeed are the references to clothes in the contemporary records of this time, although we find that the Scots, a wild and somewhat conservative race regarding clothes, took exception to what they considered effeminacy in the attire of their English enemies. Notices were pinned up on church doors about the fashions and manners of the English. One at St. Peter's, Stangate, was as follows:

> " Long beards heartleſſe,
> Painted hoods witleſſe,
> Gay coats graceleſſe
> Makes England thriftleſſe ! "

The long beards must have been a fleeting fashion, as there seems to be a scarcity of beards, either long or short, between 1330 and 1350. Painted hoods and hats were worn from about 1325, and embroidered and hand-painted materials were popular throughout the century. The " gay coats " referred to were in all probability the parti-coloured garments, a fashion which survived, in hose at least, until the time of the Tudors.

The costume of a man of the time consisted of the following garments. Firstly the shirt, an undergarment and rarely visible; over this was worn the doublet, or gipon, as it was then called. The gipon was a closely-fitting tunic reaching to the knees, and its tightly-fitting sleeves were usually visible under the cotehardie, or external garment. The hose were separate, like the stockings of to-day, and were tied to the gipon with a multitude of strings. Hoods were worn by practically everyone; sometimes they were attached to cloaks, but more often were a separate garment confining the head and shoulders, with a circular aperture for the face.

1325—1350 (*continued*)

It was towards the middle of the century that English life began to recover some of its animation. Commerce and extended trade in woollen manufacture helped to enrich a nation impoverished and spiritless after a succession of long and costly wars. Prosperity had an immediate effect on costume. The somewhat meaningless draperies of the early fourteenth century took on the clinging lines associated with the costume of the Middle Ages, and dignity and grace appeared where only utility and economy had found a place.

Patterns, though simple in design, were often woven into the materials, and richly ornamented girdles and belts were worn by both men and women. Buttons of fantastic design played an important part in the decoration of gowns and cotehardies, and tassels and cords appeared on cloaks. In fact, the whole order of attire gradually took on more importance and interest.

It was during the 'thirties that the "dagged" fashion first became so popular. The term "dagged" or "jagged" means the cutting away of the edges of garments to form a pattern. Sometimes scalloped or pointed, the fashion offered great scope for individual feelings and requirements, and it soon spread to other garments, even appearing on the tops of boots and shoes. Excellent examples of "dagged" garments may be seen on the figures on contemporary tombs, although it is unfortunate that practically all the men of the period chose to have their effigies representing them in full armour. However, there are a few of children and youths and many of ladies that show, perhaps better than any other records, what beautiful lines appeared in the long dagged sleeves, and the graceful fullness of cloaks and gowns.

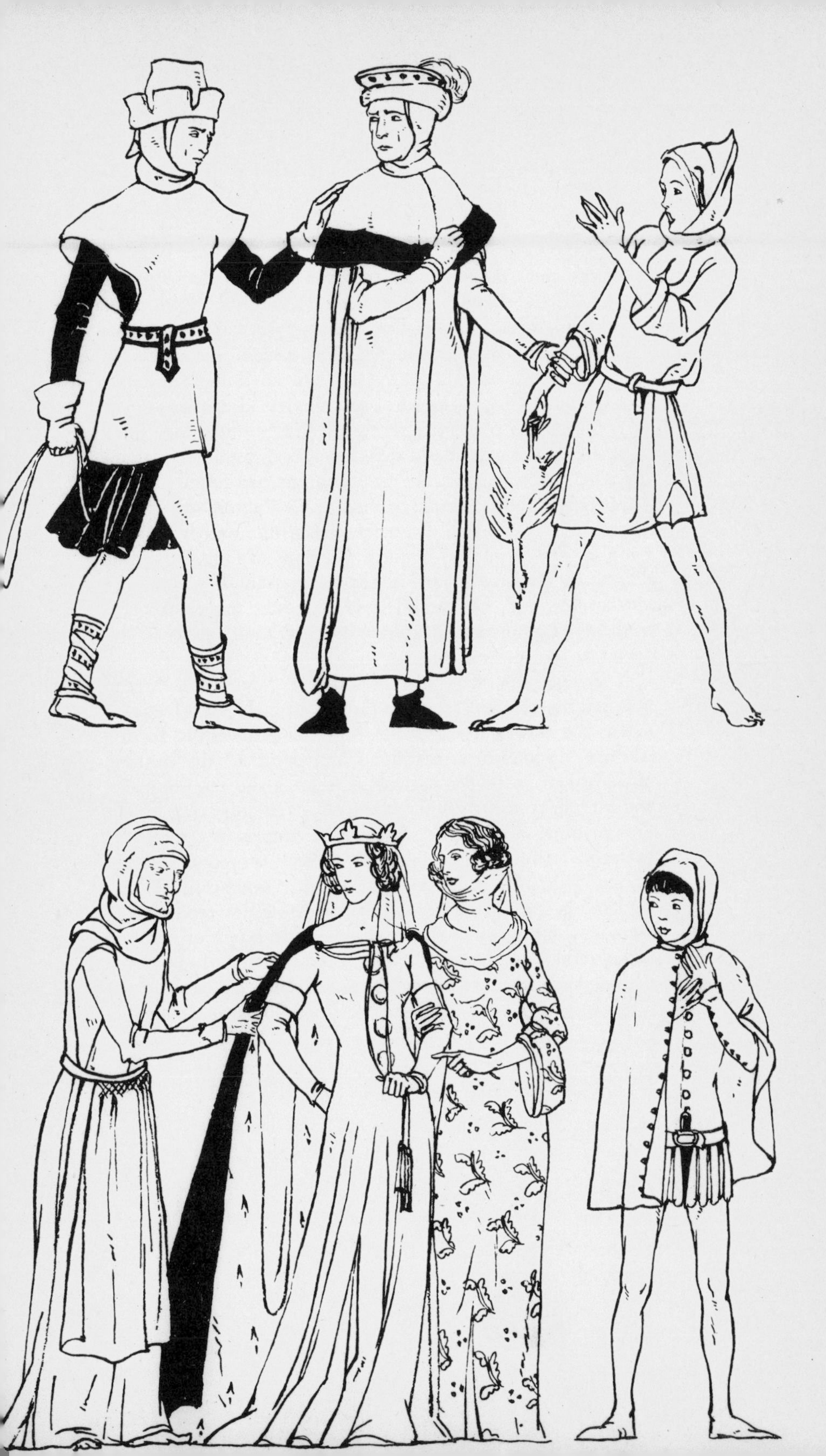

1325—1350 (*continued*)

The wimple was worn throughout the century, and the barbette, or band under the chin, which might be attached to the plaits at the side of the face or draped right round the face, was to be seen until the 'seventies. The veil and circlet, or crown, are typical of the fourteenth century. No woman's head was dressed without a veil of some description, either draped round her chin or worn over her head, or both. A gilded or jewelled circlet or an ornate net was also worn. Head-dresses constituted almost the only extravagance permitted to women at this period. While crowns or circlets were worn by the wives and daughters of noblemen, veils, nets, barbettes, and hoods were worn by all.

Women's clothes at this time fitted the figure closely to the hips and then splayed out into a wealth of graceful folds. The kirtle or under-gown was very tight-fitting, with sleeves buttoned from wrist to elbow. The surcoat worn over this was sometimes cut away at the sides in order to display a jewelled hip-belt. Occasionally the surcoat had sleeves to the elbow, and a tippet was worn. The tippet in this case was a band of contrasting material or fur, varying in length from a few inches to several feet, sewn round the arm, and allowed to hang from the elbow.

So scarce are the records of this time that, with the exception of the Loutrell Psalter and the Queen Mary Psalter, almost the only examples of English wearing apparel are to be found on tombs and wall-paintings. It is a great loss to students of contemporary fourteenth-century decoration to find that a number of valuable sources have been defaced or removed during the last hundred and fifty years. There are a few books printed at the beginning of last century which give tantalising glimpses of figures on tombs which no longer exist. Unfortunately these sketches are hardly sufficient as a basis for reliable detail.

1325—1350 (*continued*)

It is interesting to note that in the year 1339 Edward III received thirty thousand pounds from duties levied on the exportation of wool. The king's hold on Flanders at this time was largely due to the fact that, had this exportation ceased, half the population of the large Flemish towns would have been unemployed. Shortly after he invited Flemish weavers to take up their residence in England, and looms were set up in the eastern counties, especially Kent, and from the middle of the fourteenth century onwards woollen fabrics were woven in England.

The wealthy continued to wear silk and velvet and cloth of gold imported from abroad, but the less affluent welcomed the new woollen materials with joy and delight.

The figures on the opposite page are as typical as any of this particular twenty-five years. The hood and dagged gorget worn by the man were seen in hundreds of slightly different variations during this period, and so were the tight-sleeved kirtle, and button and tippet-trimmed surcoat worn by the woman. The veil, loosely worn over the plaited hair, was possibly the simplest method of head-dressing at this time, and certainly very charming. The simple spot pattern on her gown has been taken from a contemporary design, and if not actually woven into the material, was hand-embroidered. Some of the exquisite embroidery on the dresses of this period must have taken half a lifetime to execute, and it is fortunate in this age of leisure that by the time the embroidery was finished the gown was not too old-fashioned to wear.

1350—1375

THE difference between the attire of the ordinary people and that of the nobility was more noticeable in the men's attire than in the women's. The citizen's wife might wear a dress almost identical with one worn in the household of a knight, differing only in the apron and probably the wimple worn by the citizen's wife, and the coronet and veil and possibly the cloak worn by the knight's wife.

The vogue for embroidery spread to the homes of all, and many long hours were spent in work of this kind. Bands of simple design were to be seen at the neck and hem, and often on the sleeves, of practically all feminine attire.

The power of the Church at this time seems to have been quite negligible as regards sobriety and modesty in clothes. It is particularly interesting to note this when it is realised that priests and nuns all wore the same attire as their brothers and sisters who had not taken holy orders. The court of Edward III was singularly unhampered by the disapproval of the Church, and the extravagance and vice of the nobility was reflected in their dress.

A contemporary writer, disgusted by a recent exhibition at a tournament, gives a good description of the fashionable male attire worn during the 'sixties: "Whenever there was a tournament there came a great concourse of ladies of the most costly and beautiful, but not of the best in the kingdom, sometimes forty or fifty in number, as if they were a part of the tournament, in diverse and wonderful male apparel, in parti-coloured tunics, with short caps and bands wound round their head, and girdles bound with gold and silver, and daggers in pouches across their body . . ."

1350—1375 (*continued*)

Although it was not until the 'eighties that William Langland wrote the *Complaint of Piers Plowman*, the social conditions which he so vividly describes were very much the same as in the 'seventies, and the contrast between the poor working man and the wealthy churchman was as great.

His description of the ploughman shows how pitiful and poverty-stricken was his condition :

" His cote was of a cloute, that cary was y-called,
His hood was full of holes, and his hair oute,
With his knopped schon (shoes) clouted full thykke . . .
His hosen overhangen his hokschynes, on each side . . ."

He also speaks of the friars wearing spotless linen underneath their outer garments, which were so dirty that corn might be grown in them ! The cotton cope which covered them was only an outward sign of endurance, for beneath this they were well-padded with short fur or beaver coats, and socks were surreptitiously worn inside the shoes to keep their feet from chilblains. Piers Plowman's bitterness is further increased by the fact that the clergy asking for alms in the street were often the proud possessors of six or even seven copes, and could afford the luxury of red shoes.

It was at about this time that regulations for moderation in the garments of the Grey Friars were issued : " Bredth of hood not wider than the shoulder bone, length of gown not longer than its wearer, bredth not more than sixteen spans, nor less than thirteen. The sleeves over the joint of the finger and no furthur. The mantles must be of vile and coarse cloth not curiusly made or pynched about the neck."

1375—1400

THE closing quarter of the century held the greatest changes in costume. With the marriage of Richard II and Anne of Bohemia in 1383 the court became a centre of luxury, and the royal couple were leaders of the exaggerated fashions which prevailed. Anne brought with her a variety of previously unknown ideas regarding clothes, the most important being the gigantic and ornate head-dresses, which were worn throughout the following century, increasing in size as the century advanced.

It was a period of fantastic costume, the beginning of the ornate and decorative attire that is always associated with the Middle Ages. The houppelande, a gown made in a bell shape, with a hole for the neck in the centre of the circle, made its appearance during the 'eighties. This was worn by both men and women, and was cut in varying lengths to suit the wearer. The feminine edition was usually cut with a large aperture at the neck, and was held with a wide belt, usually embroidered, which reached from the waist to close under the breasts; this new high waist was definitely revolutionary, and its popularity almost exceeded that of the surcoat cut away at the sides.

The masculine houppelande was high-necked, often covering the ears. Sometimes the garment only reached the thighs, but often it fell in increasing fullness to the ankles. Houppelandes were worn right through the following century, and the gracefulness of the heavy folds was an outstanding feature of the dress of the Middle Ages. At a later date the folds were sewn in to the waist, giving the skirt a more formal effect.

The man's hood on the opposite page is of the separate type, which was not as popular as those which enveloped the face and shoulders. His surcoat is the houppelande with the now popular bell-shaped sleeves. This type of sleeve, turned back and lined with contrasting material, and allowing the sleeves of the doublet beneath to be seen, remained in fashion throughout the following century. The jewelled girdle not only encircles the waist, but it also holds together the front of the skirts. The shoes are typical of perhaps a few years earlier; the fashion of embroidering and bejewelling went out with the arrival of the exaggerated long-toed shoes. The girl's dress is definitely earlier than the arrival of Anne of Bohemia, probably about 1380.

1375—1400 (*continued*)

Chaucer gives an excellent description of the houppelande in his picture of the friar :

> " Of double worsted was his semi-cope,
> That round was, as a belle, out of the presse."

There are many allusions to clothes in the history of this period—partly because of the new importance attached to them by the court, and partly because the people found in them an excellent opportunity for pointing a finger at the extravagance of their oppressors. John Ball, " a mad priest of Kent," as Froissart calls him, protested strongly at the wilful waste and unbridled extravagances of the rich : " They are clothed in velvets and rich stuffs, ornamented with ermine and other rich furs, while we are forced to wear poor cloth." Another interesting note is that Wat Tyler bought sixty doublets for his men at the amazingly low price of thirty marks, and incidentally never paid for them !

It was during the 'eighties that women first rode side-saddle ; previously they had all ridden astride like men, with their skirts tucked into a bag-like affair.

The toes of shoes became even more exaggerated in length than before ; the points were often tied to the knees with gold or silver chains to avoid the possibility of the wearer tripping over them.

A wealth of colourful description is to be found in Chaucer's *Canterbury Tales*. His brilliant portrayal of the numerous pilgrims leaves little to the imagination as to their appearance. Perhaps the most curious thing to us about all these descriptions is the importance placed upon the pouches, knives, and jewellery ; these etceteras obviously played a very important part in the attire of the well-dressed.

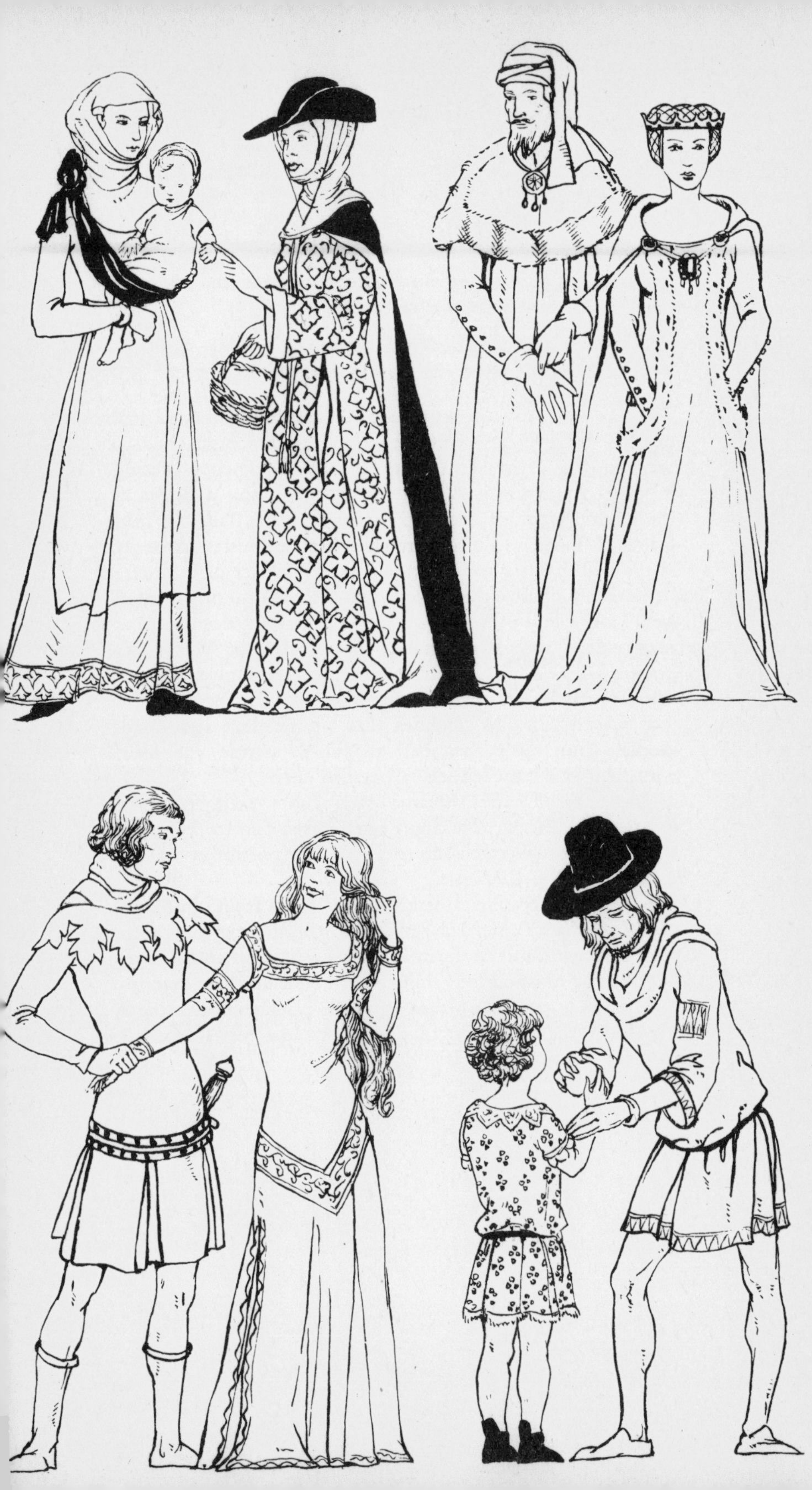

1375—1400 (*continued*)

We read that the Wife of Bath wore scarlet hose, that the Merchant wore a " Flaundrish bever hat," and that the young Squire wore his hair curled and

" Embroidered was he, as it were a mead
All ful of fresshe flowers, white and red."

The 'Mellere' wore a " Whit cote and a blew hood "; we read of the 'Reeve' that:

" His beard was shave as nigh as ever he can,
His heer was by his eres round i-shorn.
His top was dockèd lyk a priest biforn.
Ful longe were his legges, and ful lene,
Al like a staff, ther was no calf y-sene.
. . . . . .
A long surcote of blew uppon he hadde,
And by his side he bar a rusty blade."

A long description of hairdressing is given in the picture of the Pardoner:

" This pardoner had heer as yellow as wex,
But smothe it hung, his lokkes that he hadde,
And therwith he his shuldres overspredde.
Full thinne it lay, in lengthes, one by one,
And hood, for jolitte, werèd he none,
For it was trussèd up in his wallet.
He thought he rode al of the newe set,
Disheveled, save his cappe, he rode all bare."

The Sergent of Lawe " rode but hoomly in a medly cote,
Girt with a girdle of silk, with barres smale ! "
And the Doctor of Phisik
" In blue he clad was al and sangwyn
Lynèd with taffeta and silke thin."

1375—1400 (*continued*)

There is no doubt that the works of Chaucer are, from the costume point of view, unrivalled in valuable detail. With the possible exception of some of the Diaries of the seventeenth century, no other contemporary source of any period provides us with such a wealth of interesting and valuable data as to modes and manners of the times. Not only does Chaucer describe the general appearance of his characters, but he gives also minute descriptions of materials, colours, and fashions in jewellery and hairdressing, and other interesting details which the more staid chroniclers of history fail to record.

References to some of the more exaggerated clothes of the period are to be found in several of John Wyclif's tracts. The wealthy churchmen, who paraded themselves in exaggerated sleeves, costly materials, and curled hair, was no light matter, and the delicious humour to be found in the writings of his contemporary find no place in Wyclif's writings. Little escaped Chaucer's quick eye, and he records all the minor points of detail in the Monk's costume:

> "I saw his sleves rounded at the hand
> With fur, and that the fynest in the land.
> And for to fastne his hood under his chyn
> He hadde of gold y-wrought a curious pyn:
> A love-knotte in the gretter ende ther was."

The number of references to jewellery made by Chaucer indicates what an important part it played in the costume of the period. Even the nun had her share of personal adornment:

> "Ful faire was her robe, as I was war.
> Of smal corál aboute her arme she bare
> A paire of bedes, the greatest were of grene;
> And theron hung a broch of gold ful shene,
> On which was first i-writ a crownèd A,
> And after, *Amor vincit omnia*."

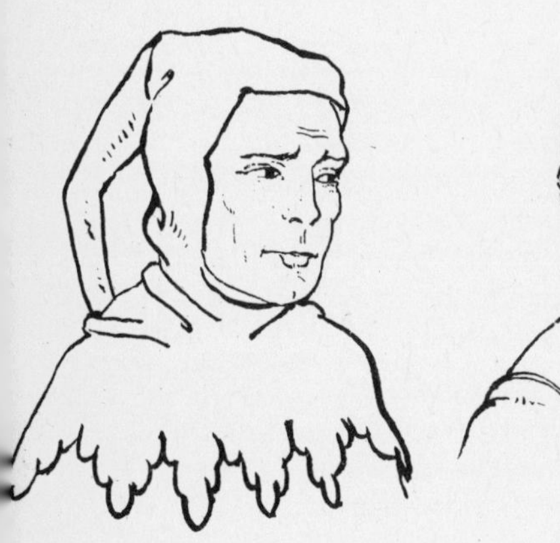

1400—1420

THE manuscripts, both illuminated and illustrated, of this century, show a wealth of beautiful detail in both colour and line, but unfortunately there was no one to take Chaucer's place, and descriptions of costume are sadly lacking. As many of the manuscripts took twenty years or more to execute, it is difficult to estimate with any strict exactitude the date of the costumes illustrated, although a number of minor, if not major, changes in style over a period of twenty years help to decide within ten years or so the date of the dress.

It should be remembered, too, that the fashions at court changed slowly, and took a long time to filter down to the country, and that the garments had a long life ; thus it is possible to realise why a particular gown may be almost identical with one of fifty or sixty years earlier.

The most obviously new innovation of this period was the short doublet. The hose had been cut to reach the waist, possibly as much as fifteen or twenty years earlier, and gradually the skirts of the outer garment became more and more brief, until they were eventually merely a pleated frill some six inches below the waist.

The houppelande in its most exaggerated forms, with sleeves almost as full as the gown itself sweeping the ground, was a favoured garment for those wishing to appear more dignified and prosperous than those who favoured the absurdly abbreviated tunics. Two so entirely dissimilar fashions have rarely appeared together in the history of costume.

1400—1420 (*continued*)

Variety and exaggeration in dress seem to have been general tendencies at this time; she who could outdo her neighbour in the size of head-dress and the width of skirts would deem the effort well worth while. The young squire of the day spent his all on the latest thing in embroidered surcoats and painted hoods, and went to great pains that his hair should at least be as well curled as his neighbour's. According to the miniatures of the period the hair was often crimped, giving the effect of having been tightly plaited and then undone. It is possible, however, that this was the contemporary interpretation of curly hair, and that all the young squire did was to plait his locks tightly overnight. Chaucer's Squyer, " with lokkes curled as if they lay in presse," rather gives us this impression.

Several new styles of sleeve made their appearance at the beginning of the fifteenth century. Where previously only the tight-fitting and the bell-shaped, or a combination of the two, had been worn, there were now sleeves of practically every known shape and size. The new bagpipe sleeve, made like a gigantic bag, fitting at the shoulder and hanging in loose folds to be gathered into a tight band at the wrist, was popular for a few years. Two examples of this may be seen on the opposite page, that at the bottom being a very subdued version. The surcoat was often worn with a sleeve to the elbow, and an example of the tippet worn at the wrist of the gipon may be seen on the last figure on the page.

The tight sleeve with a roll or gathered puff at the shoulder was worn more often with the short-skirted garment. All sorts of varieties in the arrangement of the bell-shaped sleeve were to be seen; sometimes the sleeve was turned back to the elbow, showing a fur lining; sometimes it was gathered into a bunch at the shoulder and left to fall in deep folds under the arm. Some sleeves were so excessively long and full that the lower parts were tied in great knots to save them dragging along the ground.

1400—1420 (*continued*)

Few indeed were the garments worn at this time that were not either embroidered or patterned in some manner or other ; even when plain cloth was used it was decorated with bands of embroidery or fur. The passion for decorating even extended to the tops of hose. Tapestry-like embroideries were seen on almost every woman's gown. Embroidery had ceased to be merely a matter of spot patterns ; most of the designs were large, and were often repeated only two or three times on a garment. The designs seem to have been arranged after the garments were made, as often the central floral or imaginative motif appears on the front of a gown, with the rest of the design merely emphasising it. In smaller designs the motif appears symmetrically on the shoulders and in the middle of the back.

When spot patterns were used, they were usually larger and more dignified than those in vogue during the previous century, but their popularity waned as the century proceeded, and they made way for the boldness and exaggeration which was characteristic not only of design. Indeed, boldness and exaggeration, combined with a sense of dignity, typifies the outlook on costume during the greater part of the fifteenth century. Hardly a single fashion was introduced that was not carried to one extreme or another after it had been in vogue for a few years.

Literature had fallen to a very low level ; Chaucer was dead, and there was no one to record for posterity the life and work of the time ; indeed, almost the only literary productions were pamphlets and rhyme-sheets, and translations of French romances, which appeared in large numbers. From the point of view of costume they are quite useless, and if it were not for the letters of the Paston family it would be difficult to bridge the gap. Their letters are invaluable, and contain many details and descriptions of costumes and materials in use between 1420 and 1500.

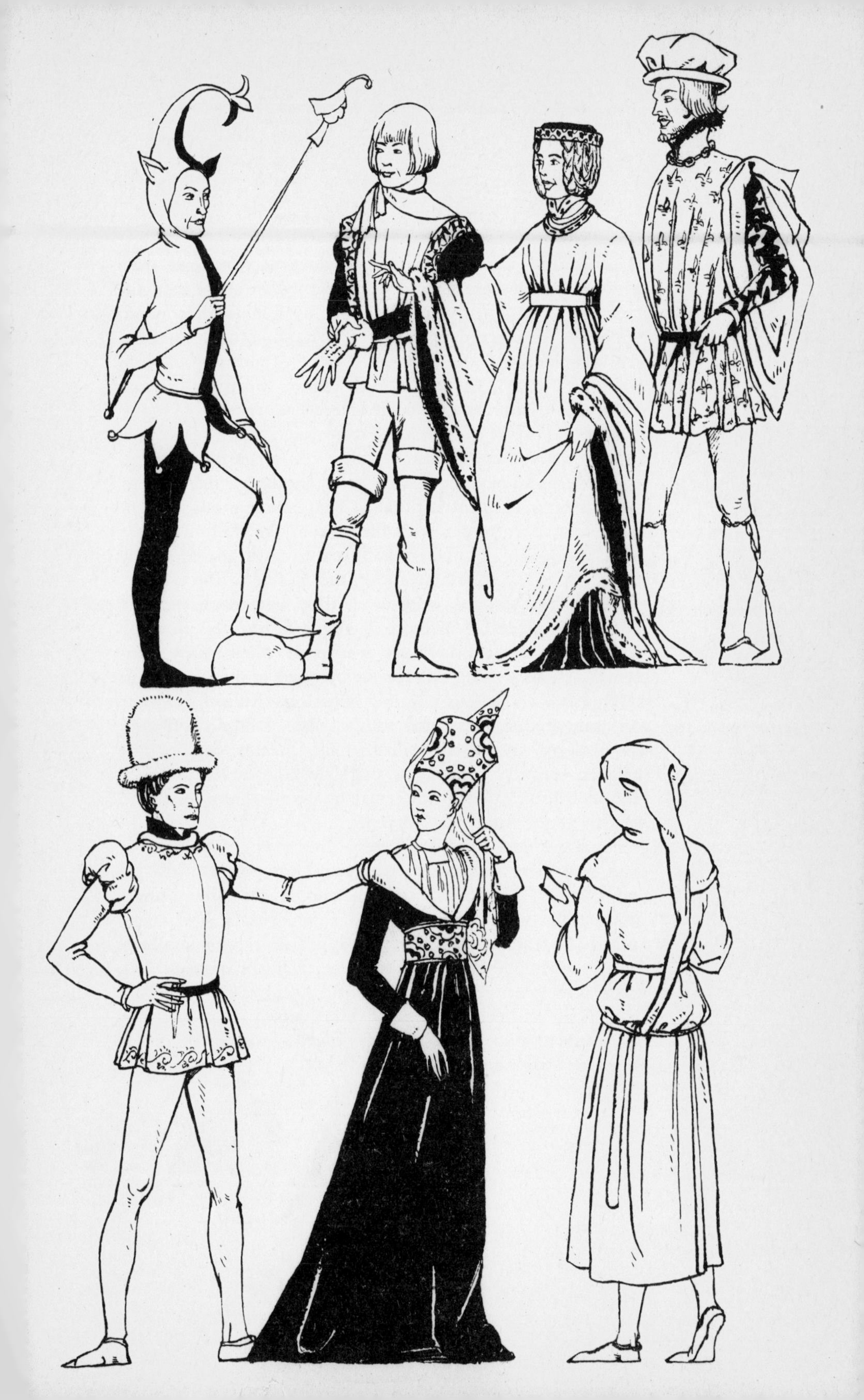

1400—1420 (*continued*)

Head-dresses were already tall and ornate, but they became more and more exaggerated. The head-dress assumed more importance, and in order that nothing should distract attention from it, it became the fashion to pluck the hair on the forehead and on the back of the neck. It was a common sight to see ladies of fashion plucking their necks in public with the aid of a small mirror or a piece of polished metal. It was not considered any more remarkable than it is now for a woman to be seen powdering her nose or adding a touch of lipstick in a 'bus or drawing-room.

The illustration opposite shows the horned head-dress, completely covered with a veil. The simple lines of the dress are an excellent background for the amazing quantity of fur lavished on the immense sleeves. It is interesting to note that the man is wearing chains attached below the knee, to which the toes of his shoes may be tied. His short gown has the bagpipe sleeves already mentioned, and a " harness " is slung across the shoulder. Often these " harnesses " had bells attached. In the manuscript from which this costume is taken the gown is white, with a bold green and pink design; the hat scarlet, with a gold coronet. The habit of wearing a crown on the hat was practised a great deal by royalty and the nobility.

1400—1420 (*continued*)

By 1420 the gipon was made with the high collar, and the surcoat was cut low at the neck to reveal the contrasting colour of the collar beneath. Usually the outer gown had the neck cut in a V-shape behind, and was edged with fur.

Large beaver hats, and those made of velvet and cloth, were almost as much worn as the hood, which by this time differed a great deal from its original form. The cockscomb effect was more frequently seen than previously, and the liripipe had now assumed the title of tippet. A "tippet" at this time seems to have been the name used for practically all pieces of material that were depended from the main garment.

The steeple head-dresses assumed a gigantic height during the 'twenties and 'thirties; the veil was elongated, and was often worn over the arm to prevent it trailing the ground. It was about this time that the rather attractive eye-veil was added to this type of head-dress. The head-dress like a flower-pot on the opposite page, worn with a veil under the chin and a tie at the top, was not seen later than the 'forties. It was not nearly so popular as the steeple, horned or rolled head-dresses, examples of which are seen from the end of the fourteenth to the end of the fifteenth centuries.

It is interesting to compare the simplicity of the woman's bonnet or hood at the bottom of the page with the complicated head-dresses worn at this time. It appears to be made from a perfectly straight piece of material folded in half and sewn down the back only, the front part being cut and turned back at the face.

1420—1440

THE extravagant use of furs throughout the fifteenth century gives the impression that England was rich in animals. Much fur was imported, but it was obviously too expensive to be used profusely except by the wealthy; the others had to content themselves with home-cured fur.

The man's gown on the page facing is cut at the sides, front, and back to facilitate riding, and is obviously lined with fur throughout. The lady's gown is richly trimmed with ermine; the tippets on her sleeves are exaggerated into a double-skinned and voluminous drapery hanging from a band at the elbow, the end narrowing so that it may be tied round the wrist should it prove too heavy or cumbersome. It will be noticed that the box-like head attire is surmounted by a circlet of an irregular diamond shape. These circlets were also worn on top of the horned head-dress.

Shoes with extremely exaggerated toes were not so popular as they had been a few years earlier. The fashion of attaching chains to the toes of the shoes, mentioned a few pages earlier, had proved to be unsatisfactory. It was quite impracticable, and when people found it was difficult for them to walk a few steps, and impossible to walk upstairs, the craze soon died out.

The taste for fantastic clothing spread to people of all classes, which so little pleased the nobility that laws were introduced restricting those with an income of less than forty pounds a year from indulging in the most extravagant fashions. Gowns and jackets had to cover the buttocks, and the pikes on shoes were to be no longer than two feet in length!

1420—1440 (*continued*)

Men, as well as women, wore elaborate headgear, and their immense hats were exaggerated and ornamented to an absurd extent. The fashion for decorating the crowns of hats was first indulged in soon after the middle of the fourteenth century, but a more orthodox brim than that shown on the opposite page was then worn. Gigantic soft-crowned hats, like an electric bulb in shape, another like a three-tiered turban, and numerous other queer and exaggerated shapes, are to be seen in contemporary illustrations.

Indeed, there seems to be no limit to the variety of head-dresses termed fashionable. Fringes for men were very popular at this time; the hair was still curled and worn long, although it was often cut in a fringe all round, slanting up from the nape of the neck at the back, covering the tops of the ears at the sides, and merely an inch or so less in length on the forehead. It is curious that at a period when women tucked their hair out of sight, plucked their eyebrows, and sometimes, if we are to believe contemporary portraits, cut their eyelashes, that men should wear their hair frizzed and curled, and in elaborate fringes.

Tall, soft leather boots were worn for riding, either reaching well up the thighs or only half-way up the shins. In both cases they were turned back at the top and were often lined with a contrasting colour. Spurs were always used for riding, even on shoes and soled hose.

Although the illustrations on the opposite page do not show a variety of patterned materials, practically everything was richly embroidered, usually with large and somewhat irregular designs.

1420—1440 (*continued*)

The costumes depicted on the opposite page have all been specially selected to show the more sober and less exaggerated costumes worn by the older and more dignified people of the age. With the exception of the large bold designs on the materials they have little in common with the extravagant attire of the fashionable. Their somewhat sombre simplicity is in sharp contrast to the youthful and flippant garments illustrated on the previous page.

The central figure at the top of the page shows the more sober version of the horned head-dress. The horns are merely padded points over the ears, and are used as a support for the veil, which is trimmed with gathered or rouched material. Heavy gathered rouching was very fashionable for trimming, and was to be seen on even the most sober garments. Fur of all kinds was lavishly used, both for gowns and hats, and often the complete hat would be made of fur.

Small children at this time rarely wore more than a short tunic, unless they were fully clothed as miniature men and women for some very special occasion. Many examples, however, are to be seen of the very youthful page clad in an abbreviated X-shaped tunic, his long shapely legs in hose, his hair well crimped, and with a short, almost invisible, fringe peeping from beneath his flower-pot hat.

The central figure at the bottom of the page shows the method employed to fasten the hose to the gipon, when as often happened the hose were not cut to reach the waist.

The shoes illustrated are of the more useful type, some resembling a modern bedroom slipper, others consisting of a sole of leather sewn on to the hose itself.

1420—1440 (*continued*)

By the 'thirties head-dresses had assumed gigantic and imposing proportions. Many of these amazing conceptions can be seen on the figures on contemporary tombs, where a detailed and relief study will reveal far more than any sketch can possibly show. Both this and the colour drawing on page 59 are based on the same idea. This example, with the addition of horns beneath the coronet, makes it one of the most weird and wonderful head adornments of the time.

The surcoat worn by this lady has the sides cut away until merely a small strip of fur-edged material supports the skirt. The dark kirtle worn beneath is made almost skin-fitting in its tightness.

Both these figures show the lavishness of the extremes of fashion at this time. The man, with his curled hair, huge beaver hat, laced doublet, bunched shoulders and striped hose, was the gallant or fop of his period. Men's waists appear so small in contemporary portraits that one wonders if any form of corset was worn. Undoubtedly belts were worn much too tight to be comfortable, to give the X-shape effect which fashion demanded in the fifteenth century.

Extravagance and exaggeration are terms which occur frequently in describing the costumes of this period, and if a detailed study of social life was within the scope of this book references to greed, lust, and selfishness would appear with equal frequency in this age, when religion meant little and sorcery and magic were believed in by all. When one of the punishments for women guilty of immoral behaviour was for their hair to be cut off to the ears, and it was scandalous for women to show an inch of leg beneath their cumbersome skirts, and the Countess of Cobham did penance for practising magic, it is not difficult to imagine why Joan of Arc was condemned as a witch and a sorceress.

1420—1440 (*continued*)

Fantastic headgear was at its height, both literally and figuratively, during the 'thirties and 'forties of the fifteenth century. There are so many types and varieties of absurdly exaggerated hats, especially those worn by the men, that one page of drawings is quite inadequate to give even a representative selection. As the less fantastic fashions must have a place in this book if it is to be of any use as a general guide to the dress of the time, several of the more modest types of hoods, hats, and other head adornments have been included in the two following pages of drawings.

The large beaver and velvet hats, the dagged or jagged gorget, and tippet, and the nightcap or coif at the bottom of the page, are three examples of the more sober forms of headgear. Headwear as an expression of personality is perhaps a limited study in these days of mass production, but in this period of the Middle Ages students of psychology would find more than enough material for study. There seemed to be hats for every mood—fantastic or frivolous, sober or learned, and every man could let himself go in creating a model more exaggerated, more ornate, and more complicated in design than that of his neighbour. For a few years at least the men refused to be outdone by the women in the matter of head-dress; even the originally simple hood was exaggerated out of all recognition, the tippet, now wide and embroidered, often trailed the ground, the gorget fell in a profusion of ornamented folds over the shoulders, and the roll or brim assumed a stiffened and enlarged appearance.

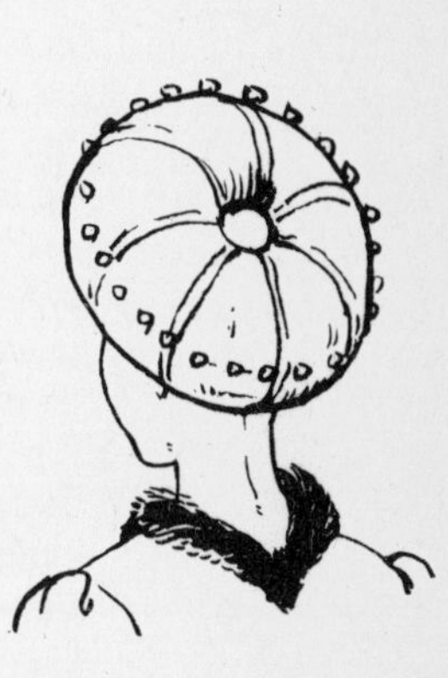

1420—1440 (*continued*)

The rolled head-dresses worn by the women at this time might take practically any shape. Instead of merely forming a frame for the face, as it did at first, it was now a joined affair, making a padded circle of any size to suit the wearer. Sometimes they were like a lifebelt in shape, and worn without a veil; sometimes the pad was exaggerated to a couple of yards in circumference, and bent into a variety of shapes. Heart-shapes and U-shapes were particularly popular. The front part was usually worn low on the forehead, and the sides lifted to show the fretted nets over the ears. As these rolls were often arranged eighteen inches or so above the head, it was fortunate that the architecture of the time allowed for this exaggerated height of headgear, and that the low beams of a few years later had not yet appeared.

The knobs on the head-dress of this period are particularly absurd, and it seems that if a head-dress was not considered sufficiently fantastic to please its owner, the addition of a knob on the top made amends for any other deficiency in the imagination of the wearer, if not in the eye of the beholder.

The influence of the East is very noticeable in the turban-like head-dresses worn by both men and women. The advancements and refinements of Eastern civilization were being gradually introduced to the West, and almost every European country imported silks and rugs, and exquisite pieces of workmanship, to grace the halls of the wealthy and to adorn their noble personages. The beautiful and exotic colours of the materials had a great and lasting effect on the costumes and decorations of the period to follow.

1440—1460

IN the year 1440 there is an interesting letter written by Agnes Paston to her husband, asking him to do some purchasing for her and her sister. "... Yil ye woulde byen her a goune, here moder Yeve ther to a godely furre. The goune nedyth for to be had; and of colour it woulde be a godely blew, or erlys a bryghte sangueyn. I prey you do byen for me ij pypys of gold." In modern English this means that her sister wanted a gown well-trimmed with fur, either blue or bright red, and that she herself would be obliged if he would buy her two reels of gold thread for embroideries.

Colours and materials at this time were of the richest, and most brilliant; velvets, damasks, figured satins, linen, keyrse, blanket musterdevelys, tisshew, cloth of gold, and cloth of silver, camlet, morey, frieze taffeta, and broadcloth, were materials most worn. Musterdevelys was a greyish soft woollen cloth, and was worn until about the middle of the sixteenth century; camlet was a heavy cloth made of camel's-hair, and exceedingly expensive.

Cloth of gold was not to be worn by any one lower than a lord's estate; neither was the use of sable permitted to any one without a title. These restrictions and others previously mentioned limiting the luxuries of dress and the extremes of fashion to certain classes seem to have been disregarded in many cases. We find, for instance, mention of two gowns of cloth of gold in the wardrobe of Sir John Falstolf in 1459.

It was during the 'forties and 'fifties of the fifteenth century that costumes reached the peak of exaggeration.

1440—1460 (*continued*)

A wealth of description of clothing is to be found in the Will of Sir John Falstolf. It is impossible to include all the details, and space can only be found for some of the more interesting data :

"First, a gown of cloth of gold, with side sleeves surplis wise.

Item 1. Another gown of cloth of gold, with straight sleeves and lined with black cloth.

Item. Half a gown of red velvet.

Item. Gown of blue velvet upon velvet long furred with martyns and trimmed of same, sleeves single.

Item. Red gown of Lord Cornwall's livery, lined.

Item. Gown cloth of green 3 yards.

Item. Side scarlet gowns not lined.

Item. Chammer cloak (one cut in the centre) of blue satin, trimmed with black silk."

Among his numerous jackets we find one : "The brest and slevs of blak felwett, and the remnant of russet fustian."

Some of the detailed descriptions of the hoods are extremely interesting : "Hode of blakke velvet, with a typpet half damask half velvet y-jagged." Another : "Hode of depe grene velvet, jagged upon the rolle," and another was "of russet velvet, with a typpet half of the same and half blew velvet, lined with blew damask."

There is yet another of purple velvet without roll or tippet. The tippet in this case referred to the appendage which had once been the liripipe and now hung from the roll in a profusion of folds.

The "Items" mentioned above are only a small proportion of the garments described in the Will. This gentleman owned doublets, petticoats (skirts), jackets, gowns, hoods, etc., in profusion, mostly in velvets and other rich stuffs.

1440—1460 (*continued*)

It will be noticed that from time to time one of the pages in each group of costumes is mainly devoted to the less exaggerated costumes of the period, and the page facing illustrates the more sober fashions of the time. It is not easy to maintain a sense of proportion; the extremes and extravagances more readily attract the eye, and contemporary sources usually give only the more exaggerated interpretations of costume and neglect the less spectacular garments of the period.

The huge bell sleeve turned back at the wrist and showing the tight under-sleeve was worn by all classes. The figure of the boy at the bottom of the page shows an example of the detached sleeve tied at the shoulder with "points," and not attached to the gown under the arm. The sleeve of the gipon underneath is slit up to the shoulder and tied in a number of points, revealing the shirt-sleeve beneath.

The fashion for "points," a string similar to a boot-lace, was first introduced in about the 'fifties of this century. These "points" were means of tying a slashed garment where it would best display the garment worn beneath. They became even more popular in the reign of Henry VIII, and were then seen on practically every item of male attire.

It will be noticed that the examples of dress on the opposite page have little in common with those on the previous page, where an attempt has been made to indicate the elaborate decorations of fur, embroidery, and trimming on every garment. Even the veils worn on head-dresses had spangles or rouching, or ornaments of some kind, and nothing that could be decorated seemed to escape the ever-busy needles of the ladies of quality.

1440—1460 (*continued*)

In the year 1449 Margaret Paston writes to her husband, asking him to buy her some cloth, "That ye wille do byen sume frese to in maken of your child is gwnys; ye shall have best chepe and best choyse of Hayis wyf, as it is told me. And that ye wyll bye a yerd of brode clothe of blac for an hode fore me of 44d or 33d or 4 shillings a yerd for there is no good fryse in this town."

Shopping must have been a sorry business for ladies of the time. There were few shops to be found outside the big cities, and to a large extent everyone relied on pedlars. These travelling salesmen could only carry a limited stock, and if they had nothing suitable, materials for a new gown or hood had to be purchased through the services of a relative staying or living in London.

Some time in 1445 William Paston writes to his wife, asking her if she could buy some materials for his liveries. Her reply indicates how limited were the stocks kept in the smaller towns. She writes, "As touching for your liveries, there can none be got here of that colour that ye would have of, neither murrey, nor blue, nor good russets, underneath 3 shillings a yard at the lowest price, and yet is there not enough of one cloth and colour to serve you."

1440—1460 (*continued*)

Referring again to the invaluable Paston letters, there is a complete inventory three years later of the gowns owned by Clement Paston while at Cambridge, including "A short green gown, and a short musterdeuyllers gown. A short blue gown, a long russet gown trimmed with bever, and a long murry gown." Fur was still used a great deal, and the furs most frequently used seem to be ermine, beaver, marten, bogey, and sable.

The monstrous winged head-dress did not appear until the middle of the fifteenth century. It must have a great deal of care in laundering, and as starch was unknown at this period, some difficulty must have risen in stiffening it. Probably a solution of glue or size was used. The fashion did not last so long as the still popular steeple and roll, and comparatively few examples are to be found, although one portrait of Elizabeth Woodville shows an almost obliterated version of this butterfly effect.

1460—1480

THE charming gown worn by the lady on the opposite page is of an unusual design; the scalloped bodice and the richly embroidered skirts being of different materials. The design on the skirt is taken from a contemporary miniature. Several of these bold and beautiful designs have been the inspiration for some of the modern designs found on woollen embroideries and furnishing materials sold in most of the big London shops to-day.

The long gown worn by the man has an amusing method of adornment in the three long thin cords hanging from the yoke of the gown. They were almost invisible, and although weighted with beads, they must have got constantly tangled, and altogether been an incredible nuisance. But comfort seems to have been a secondary consideration in this century, and few garments permitted the freedom we demand to-day.

It was during the 'sixties that the fashion for short cloaks for men became prevalent. They were cut in varying lengths to reach the hem of the doublet, whether the doublet reached only the waist or continued half-way down the thighs. One or two examples of this fashion are to be found on the following pages, including a very extreme example on page 73, which barely reaches the waist. It is quite obvious that this gentleman had an income of more than forty pounds a year!

1460—1480 (*continued*)

The two short gowns or jackets worn by the men at the top of the page are interesting examples of new designs. The first is worn without a belt or girdle, this being unnecessary as the pleats are sewn down tightly to the waist at the back. The doublet in this case is lower in neck-line than in previous modes. The second gown is almost armour-like in its simplicity ; cut from some stiff material, it is made up without gathers or pleats of any sort, except for the slight gathering at the shoulders, which was a necessary finish to any fashionable garment in the latter part of the fifteenth century.

At the bottom of the page will be seen a new idea in boots. The boot is cut in the usual soft leather, but fits the leg so tightly that there is no drop over at the top ; the tops are cut to form a point at each side, and a design is embroidered round the edge.

A curious version of the horned head-dress appears next to the figure in boots. The hair is drawn through the horns and falls in exaggerated waves through the extreme ends of the tubes. It is extremely unusual for the hair to be seen, as at this time every wisp of hair was tucked out of sight. The sleeves are also unusual, as no less than three garments are visible ; the under-garment with tight-fitting sleeves is the smock or shift.

The use of " points " as a means of decoration can be seen in two of the figures on this page, where they are merely tied to the upper sleeve and serve no useful purpose. The small boy's hose are tied to his abbreviated gipon, and can be seen through his sideless gown. An example of the shoes worn by women can be seen on the first figure. They were made of soft leather, and with little variation were worn throughout the century. Clogs or pattens were worn by all in bad weather, and wooden soles were worn on many shoes.

1460—1480 (*continued*)

Margery, the young wife of John Paston, was one of a type that has persisted through the centuries. In her letters to her husband during his absence from home there are constant references to the fact that she has "nothing to wear." In one letter she writes asking him to buy her a new gown, adding that "I have no gowne but my blak and my grene," and both of these she is tired of wearing. She also demands a girdle, as she has only one fit to wear, and her friend Elizabeth Peveral has at least fifteen or sixteen. Girdles at this time were very important items in a lady's wardrobe. They were of two main types: the wide ones, which were the only trimming to a simply-cut gown, and a narrower type jewelled and decorated for more elaborate gowns.

Girdles increased in importance and value, and a few years later, in the will of Dame Elizabeth Brown, several of different materials and design are bequeathed to various friends and relatives: "Three embroidered girdles, one tawny silk, with buckle and pendant, another purple, three of purple damask, some of 'tisshew,' some of 'red tisshew gold.'"

In 1471 John Paston writes home for some of his clothes, which he finds he requires: "Two long gowns, and two doublettes, and a jaket of plonket camlet, and a morey bonet out of my cofyr."

It will be noticed that the long gowns were nearly all split at the sides at this time. Formality in their folds was brought almost to the stage of pleats. The effect of bunched shoulders was sometimes obtained by merely catching the folds at regular intervals across the arm-hole, as in the back view at the bottom of the opposite page. The sleeve, with two openings, one at the elbow and one at the bottom of the sleeve, were worn a great deal, and as will be noticed in the coloured drawing on page 79, by slipping his hand through the lower opening the boy has given an entirely different arrangement to the sleeve.

1460—1480 (*continued*)

Another example of sewn pleats on a gown is to be seen here. The belt is merely an accessory, and does not hold the waist-line, as is usually the case. The sleeves are split right up the inside of the arm and can be worn either hanging loose, as seen here, or with the hand thrust through the fur-edged cuff at the bottom.

Soft cloth and velvet caps of absurd shapes were much worn by all men at this period.

It will be noticed that the steeple head-dresses have, by this time, assumed lappets reaching down to the shoulders on each side. This must have been the beginning of the gable head-dress worn at the beginning of the sixteenth century, an example of which may be seen on the last page of the book. The steeple itself was often decorated. A variety of patterns, of which the diamond one seen here was most popular, were used to adorn these sugar-loaf head-dresses.

Deep cuffs of a contrasting material were worn on the tight-fitting sleeves after the beginning of the 'sixties. Low-necked gowns were not often seen after this time, and when the V was cut too low to suit fashion's decree, modesties filled the gap at the front. This example has an interesting finish to the neck, as the effect of a collar is achieved without one being used. No girdle or belt is worn, the gown being cut to fit the figure closely at the waist. The fashion for wearing the kirtle pleated and fuller than the gown itself was carried on into the following century.

1460—1480 (*continued*)

On the opposite page may be seen the differences in the angle, height, and design of the steeple. The upper example is worn without the eye-veil, but with long exaggerated lappets decorated with jewels, and reaching well over the shoulders. The lower example is more exaggerated in height, and may be considered the extreme of the fashion. As can be seen, the hair is strained off the face, giving the head rather an egg-like appearance.

The back view next to this figure is an example of the butterfly head-dress, and shows how the ends of the material were folded and fastened at the back.

Long quills and feathers were beginning to be worn in men's hats. Pheasants' quills and others of a stiff nature were the most popular at first, but after a few years the softer types of feather took their place. These were draped round the hat or allowed to fall gracefully over the shoulder. From about 1470 until the beginning of the nineteenth century feather-trimmed hats for men never ceased to be popular.

An example of the hood worn in the original manner, but with the liripipe wound round the head and tucked in at the side, may be seen at the bottom of the page. The hood was rarely seen worn after 1465, being forsaken for caps and hats. Beaver, velvet, cloth, and wool were the most popular materials of which they were made. Even the country people preferred caps to the somewhat clumsy hoods which they had been wearing for over twenty years.

The head-dresses of the Middle Ages were gradually subsiding; the horns had gone, the ornate circlets had vanished, and soon women's head-dresses were to be referred to as "bonnets." To our modern ears this term seems quite unsuitable for the still cumbersome and ornate head-dresses.

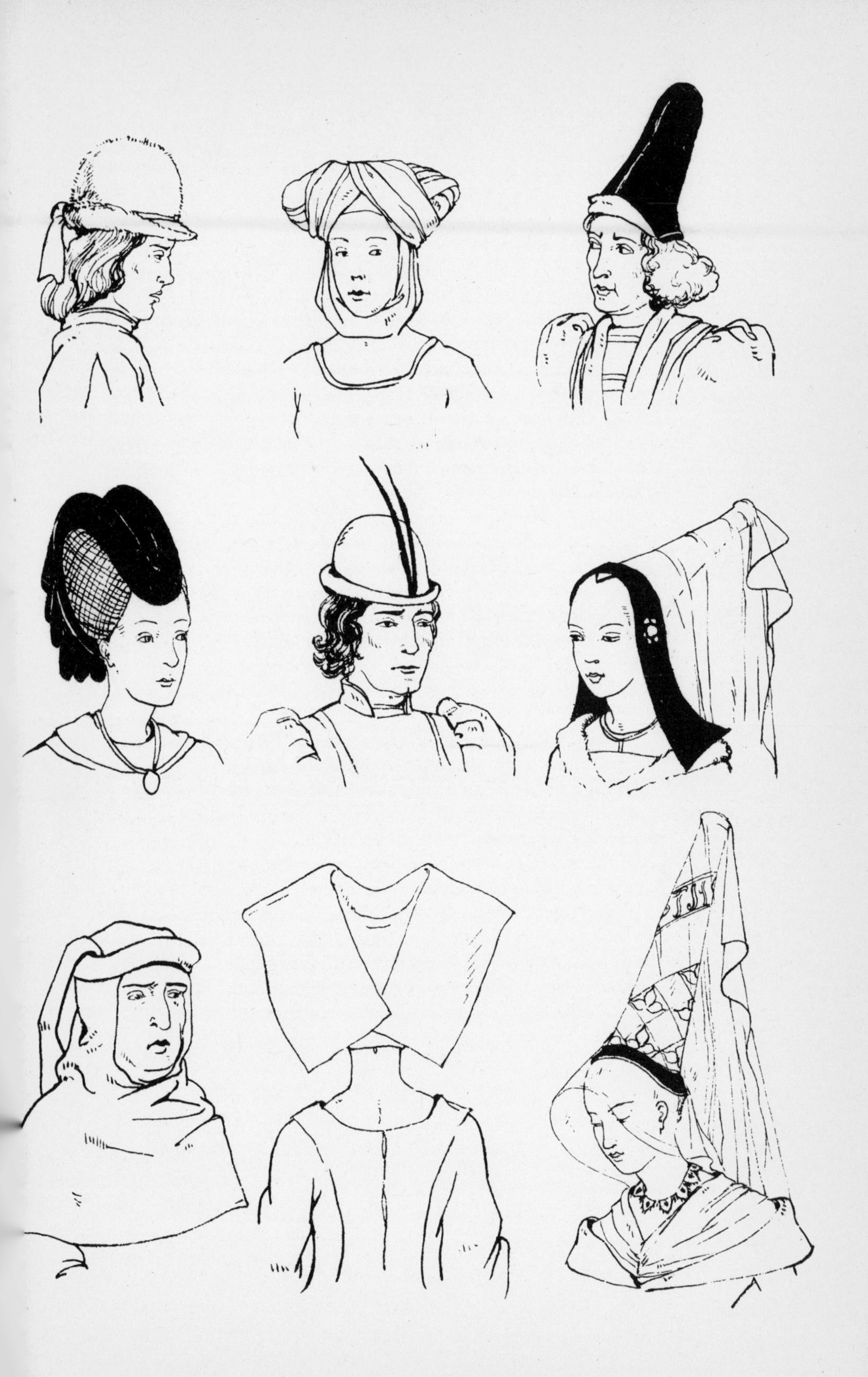

1480—1500

THE will of Dame Elizabeth Brown, referred to a few pages back, includes several details of dresses which show us how popular and important were gowns trimmed with fur. Indeed, there seem to be few garments at this time which were not either trimmed or lined with fur of one sort of another: "Violet gown furred martons, black furred with grey, black furred white, black furred martons, a kirtle of tawny chamlet, and a purfil of ermine two skins deep." The will also includes a piece of cloth of gold with dropis.

A purfil was the border or trimming at the bottom of the gown. These were obviously made separately from the gown, and attached to any gown or kirtle as required.

The sleeves of the boy's gown on the page facing have already been referred to. He is wearing one sleeve loose, and he is seen putting his hand through the cuff of fur at the bottom of the other.

The cap and hood is worn hanging down the back, with the tippet over the shoulder to keep it in place. This was frequently worn purely as an ornament, and another hat, quite separate, was worn on the head.

The girdle with the pouch at the side was a very important item of every man's attire. These pouches were almost always decorated with embroideries, beads, or painting of some sort. The long-toed shoes were not so popular as they had been throughout the earlier part of the century. They were now made almost fitting the foot, with a point an inch or so in length. The round-toed shoe was to be the fashionable shape for a few years before the arrival of the absurd square-shaped shoe of the early sixteenth century.

1480—1500 (*continued*)

Although history tells us that at this period the nobles were sorely over-taxed to fill the coffers of Henry VII, the pageantry of exotic and costly gowns and garments, of a richness and extravagance hardly rivalled by the court of Elizabeth, seems to belie this. The use of gilt and silver and the lavish use of superb and wonderful furs by the nobility and wealthy merchants hardly indicates that they were taxed to the extent of impoverishment.

The visit of the Venetian ambassador to England at the end of the century is recorded. His impressions of the country are flattering, and some of his comments on the manners and modes of the late fifteenth century amusing. " They all from time immemorial wear very fine clothes, and are extremely polite in their language. " Among other things, he is amazed to find that men take off their hats in the street as a salutation to each other.

Amongst the newer fashions are the striped and plain hose. The fashion for parti-coloured hose and for striped hose had been in vogue for many years, but the combination of one striped and the other plain was not introduced until about 1490. The man's short gown at the bottom of the page is cut away in front, revealing the pleated front of the doublet beneath. The different sleeves on this page will be noticed ; the one at the top on the right is lengthy, and though not nearly so full as those worn earlier, is considerably longer. The absurd little hats worn by the men at this time are in sharp contrast to the gigantic hoods worn a few years earlier.

Men wore their hair longer at this period, often allowing their curls to reach half-way down the back.

1480—1500 (*continued*)

It will be noticed that the outline of women's costume underwent a drastic change during the last few years of the fifteenth century. Fantastic head-dresses were no more, and the long flowing lines of the gowns of the Middle Ages gave place to the high-waisted bodices and gathered skirts of the early Tudors. The kirtle became a more important garment; and it was often made of a richer material than the gown itself, and showed several inches below the outer skirt.

The formal drapery of the head was the beginning of the coif, which became so popular during the thirty years of the following century. But perhaps the most noticeable change in women's attire was the sleeve. For so many years the tight-fitting sleeve had been regarded as a necessary foundation for another, that the new idea of wearing a comparatively loose-fitting sleeve, revealing the wrist and sometimes the lower part of the arm, must have been readily welcomed.

One last bequest of the Paston family shows the use of at least one cosmetic—face-powder. In the year 1482, Margaret Paston leaves a purple girdle harnessed with silver and gilt to her daughter Anne. A powder box, a coarse girdle of blue harnessed with silver and gilt, and beads of silver enamelled. Also to her servant, Agnes Swan, she leaves her muster-develys gown furred with black, and a girdle of black harnessed with silver and gilt and enamelled.

The references to the ornamental belts give the impression that in the last part of the fifteenth century, at any rate, they were for the most part composed of gilt or silver, and enamelled in rich colours, rather than bejewelled.

1480—1500 (*continued*)

The method of ornamentation used on the sleeves of the gown worn by the man on the page facing is extremely interesting. The pattern has been cut at the edges instead of being split, which was the usual manner of displaying the shirt sleeve beneath. The points of the pattern are tied with " points " at two places. The fur-trimmed cap, the long feathers, and the long hair are all interesting innovations.

The woman's cap, with the ears enclosed in a net and a ring on the forehead, strikes a new note when accompanied by long curls at the back, and only a small black cap, instead of a gigantic one as worn a few years earlier. The simplicity of her gown still holds something of an earlier period, and the collar and cuffs and the gathered skirt show slight indications of the fashions to come.

The clothes worn during the time of the House of York show a startling difference to those worn under the Tudors, due not to the personal endeavours of Henry VII, who had little leisure for the contemplation of fashion, but to the beginnings of the intellectual revolution of the Renaissance. Although there is little to choose between the ornateness and exaggeration of both periods, the change in general outline is remarkable. The long sweeping lines of the ladies' gowns have nothing in common with the full-skirted bunchiness of the early Tudors. The square clumsy outline of the time of Henry VIII has little in common with the somewhat effeminate fussiness of the short-skirted, long-legged, be-curled gentlemen of the previous pages. Although the clothes of the fifteenth century are perhaps less enriched with costly jewels and enamels than those worn during the sixteenth century, the wonderful colours and furs are more than recompense.

1480—1500 (*continued*)

The century closes with gorgeous pageantry. Lords and ladies arrayed in cloth of gold and ermine, with girdles of exquisite and intricate design, and decked with priceless furs and jewels, and gold and silver chains worth a king's ransom, make this period more lavish than any other in the history of English Costume.

The incredibly lovely materials, with years of work in their sight-destroying embroideries, and the wonderful examples of hand-weaving, are so dignified in their design that they make the costly materials worn a century later almost vulgar in comparison. Designs of imaginary floral figures, bold and overpowering though they were, were far more effective than the tiny naturalistic interpretations worn during the time of Elizabeth.

This last page of head-dresses shows the fusing of the old and new. The gable as it was first worn is shown; and another example was worn by widows who still clung to the wimple as a sign of mourning. The steeple at last went out of fashion about the year 1490. One or two of the ornate head-dresses of the fifteenth century were still to be seen after that date, but mostly the simpler coif and veil was favoured. Hair was to be seen once more for a few short years after a century of hiding. The small cap and long curls worn by the men show a striking contrast to the ornate, overpowering, and truly absurd erections worn on the cropped heads of fifty years earlier.

Some of the most ridiculous fashions ever worn in this country appear in this century, but they are more than balanced by some of the most charming and dignified garments ever designed to enhance the beauty of the human form.

English Costume in the Age of Elizabeth

The Sixteenth Century

FOREWORD

ALTHOUGH this book bears the title "The Age of Elizabeth," it actually covers the entire sixteenth century. To show the evolution and slow, steady development of costume it is necessary to go back to structural beginnings: the trunk-hose, the flat wool caps, and numerous other equally interesting details of dress in Elizabethan England—all had their origin in the Courts of Henry VII and Henry VIII.

Elizabeth's reign was a magnificent pageantry of exotic and fantastic costume, unrivalled in our history, which had its inspiration in the glamour of her father's Court, and owed its ultimate execution to the influx of riches into a country impoverished by recent royal extravagances. There was a notable increase in the refinements of domestic life, and with the coming of panelled rooms, latticed windows, and carpeted floors, an altogether higher degree of personal fastidiousness was displayed. Not only was more attention paid to dress, but cosmetics were introduced from the Indies, and so were several new and exciting perfumes; both these innovations tended to give a more cultivated finish to an exotic costume.

Competition, always an important factor in the history of costume, became a potent impulse, capable of greater gratification than ever before in this age when Englishmen were first journeying beyond the sea in search of commerce or adventure. A new skirt from Spain, a new hat from Italy, a hat-band from France, a slashed bombasted doublet from Germany—all were possessions to be coveted. And so it was throughout the century, each man vying with his neighbour for the possession of the greatest number and variety of enviable articles of adornment.

It is clearly impossible to illustrate here more than a small fraction of the designs that may be found in contemporary manuscripts, wall-paintings, portraits, miniatures, effigies, and actual garments still surviving. Equally impracticable would be any complete description of the minute and myriad methods of ornamentation which, in this period of most complex costume, adorned practically every item of apparel from hat to shoes. I have aimed, therefore, to condense and simplify, so that in these few hundred drawings may be found representative and typical examples of the garments which in all probability were the daily wear of our predecessors some four centuries ago.

I. B.

1520

1500—1510

WHEN the sixteenth century opened, the wealthy were spending vast sums on clothes. At the wedding of Prince Arthur and Catharine of Aragon in 1501 the Duke of Buckingham wore " a gowne wrought of needle worke and set upon cloth of tissue, furr'd with sables, the which gowne was valued at £1500. Sir Nicholas Vause, knight, wore a gowne of purple velvet dight with pieces of gold, so thick and massie that it was valued in golde besides the silke and fur a thousand pounde. Very wonderful it was to behold the riches of apparel worn that day, with puissant chaines of gold, of which two were specially noted, to wit: Sir T. Brandon, knight, master of the king's horse, which wore a chain valued at 1400 pound, and the other, W. de Rivers, esquire, master of the kinges haukes, which chain was valued at a thousand pound." And it should be realized that money then possessed quite four times its value to-day.

Men's clothes were not only costly but so rich in their variety that it is now barely possible to distinguish all their pieces as individual garments. So numerous were the additions of sleeves, skirts, fronts, and other spare parts that we cannot state definitely of what the complete costume consisted. The body-garment, however, may be assumed to have been five separate pieces. First, the shirt; here at least we are safe, for the shirt was the foundation garment and always had sleeves. It was made of holland, cambric, or lawn, and frequently it was embroidered. The neck-line was low and showed the collar-bone, occasionally so low that it scarcely covered the shoulders; more often it was round than square in cut. The sleeves were full and loose to the wrist, where they were finished with a tiny band or frill.

Over the shirt was worn the doublet, which may or may not have had sleeves. Sometimes, too, the sleeves were separate pieces tied at the shoulders with points, and showed the shirt underneath through the gaps. The doublet was usually padded and rarely reached below the waist during the first ten years of the century. Next came the jerkin or coat, similar in cut to the doublet, though it usually had sleeves of some sort, either long or to the elbow. Sometimes it was skirted, or the skirts might be entirely separate affairs, it which case they were termed *basses*.

1500—1510 (*continued*)

A gown, or more rarely a cloak, was worn over the jerkin. Usually made of some heavy woollen material and lined with fur, this could touch the ground or barely reach to the knee, as pleased its owner. Finally, men wore from the waist to the foot an entire garment—tights, hose, or stocks. These, as you may see, were simple and tight-fitting at the beginning of the century. A tendency to adorn the upper part with slashing and embroidery was the first sign of the eventual trunk-hose, predominant throughout the period. By about 1510 upper-stocks had definitely assumed the aspect of separate breeches, although actually this was not the case. These were made of cloth or velvet, cut on the cross of the material to give the necessary elasticity and stretch; knitted hose were not introduced till much later in the century.

Shoes were flat-soled, like a mule without a heel, though occasionally an inch or so of leather was added as a covering for the heel. Boots of soft coloured leather were worn for riding.

Occasionally we see examples of "rush" shoes, made of plaited straw or reeds, and worn by the peasantry. These were worn over the entire foot, and the loose ends of rush formed a rough fringe around the ankle. This type of footgear seems to have been worn extensively on the Continent, and the paintings of Hans Holbein the elder show us numerous varieties. Clogs also were not unknown on this side of the Channel.

1500—1510 (*continued*)

Women's dress, although by our modern standards distinctly complicated, was actually exceedingly simple, except in rare cases when the slashing actually cut the gown into separate parts.

First was worn the shift, similar in cut to the man's shirt; then one or two petticoats, the upper one often pleated and of a contrasting colour to the gown; then the gown itself, with full trailing skirts. In some instances the train was lifted and fastened to the girdle at the back, to show the lining, and to facilitate walking. The gown was either laced at the back or fastened in front. The neck was square and low in front, and V or U shaped at the back. Its sleeves were usually bell-shaped, with the lower edge turned back several inches to form immense cuffs which revealed the lining and displayed the sleeves underneath, which were attached to the elbow or shoulder. Plain, full sleeves, tight at the wrist, were still very popular, and there are numerous examples of tied and slashed sleeves. Also the entirely separate sleeve, tied in four or five points at the shoulder and showing the puffed shift through the gaps, was frequently worn.

Belts and girdles were a necessary part of dress for both sexes. The men had a pouch or purse hung from one side with a slit behind to hold the dagger; this fashion, however, was superseded almost at the beginning of the century by a separate sheath and dagger attached to the right-hand side of the belt. The woman's girdle was made of cord or chain, and from it hung a miscellaneous collection of household requisites, anything, in fact, from keys to a book.

Clothes were slashed, embroidered, furred, and guarded—that is, having wide bands of velvet (usually black) or embroidery sewn on the garment as a form of decoration. Precious stones, gold and silver chains and clasps, and numerous rings were worn extensively. Gloves, when worn, were cut at the knuckles to show the rings beneath.

1500—1510 (*continued*)

Male headgear might be described under two categories: the *biretta*, and the beret, very similar to that worn to-day but with a brim, usually turned up and cut in one or more places to make flaps, which frequently overlapped. Women's head-dress was less simple. The Dutch *coif*, or cap, was worn quite frequently in England. This consisted of one tight-fitting cap over the front of the head, with the hair piled up in a great coil behind it, and over this the actual *coif*, usually made of embroidered lawn. Young unmarried girls frequently wore their hair loose, or tied with a " snood," or tucked into a gold net after the French style. While the definite English tendency was for the *coif* and veil, its popularity was challenged about 1503 by the gable head-dress, which lasted with modifications for forty years or more. The gable head-dress was the roof-like arrangement worn by the second figure on the preceding page. This particular example shows the earliest type with the long side-pieces, which later were folded back across the top of the " gable." The front edge was always decorated with precious stones, and the lappets at the sides were profusely embroidered. At first the veil at the back hung down over the hair, which was loose; but later, as we shall see, the veil was split and folded back over one side of the head-dress. In the latter instances the hair seems to have been piled up under the head-dress behind, as few of these examples show us the long hair hanging down at the back.

1510—1520

FOUR hundred years ago there were no middle-classes as we know them to-day. One was either a peasant, " one of the people," or else one belonged to the nobility, which included wealthy landowners and merchants. The working people's clothes were of necessity far simpler in cut and material than those worn by their employers, and we may safely assume that for the first half of the century there was little or no change in the apparel of either men or women among the peasants.

The men wore simply a shirt and tights, the latter of cloth reaching from waist to toe, covered by a belted doublet of some rough woollen material that finished an inch or two above the knee and had long sleeves. Their boots or shoes were usually made of leather and covered the ankle. Sometimes a cloak or gown was worn for extra warmth, and the flat cap, with a brim, similar to those already described, was seen everywhere.

Peasant women wore simple woollen garments, their shifts frequently made of linsey-woolsey. The gown itself (seen in the upper drawing on p. 23) was cut with a tight bodice, sometimes laced in the front, fairly close-fitting sleeves, and a full, short skirt barely reaching to the ankles. A large apron of holland or some coarser fabric was always worn, and the belt or girdle served to carry any small article that the housewife might require from time to time. The *coif* or cap was worn throughout the period, with modifications. Women's hose were of cloth and reached just above the knee, where they were tied; shoes were of the loose slipper variety with a flat sole and round toes, and occasionally wooden shoes were worn in muddy localities.

About 1518 the " split " sleeve came into vogue for ladies of fashion. As may be seen in the costume illustrated here, the sides are caught together with gold clasps instead of the more usual " points." This mode remained in favour practically throughout the century.

1510—1520 (*continued*)

England at this period was the sole manufacturer of woollen stuffs ; therefore wool, frieze, rugge, broadcloth, kersey, and similar materials were worn extensively by all classes, although the poor frequently wove their own homespun. Only the wealthy could afford such sumptuous fabrics as cloth of gold or silver, velvet, satin, tissue, tinsel, and fine damask, which were all imported at fabulous prices from France, Spain, and Italy. About 1515 a definite German tendency prevailed in England : heavy pleating and excessive slashing are noticeable on most garments, jerkins being so closely pleated as to consist almost entirely of three layers of material. Both the jerkin and gown assumed a yoke or collar similar at the back to a sailor-collar, and to this were attached the folded edges of the pleats, leaving the fold itself free and standing out from the garment instead of sewn flat as in the modern method of pleating. Such a gown is worn by the man on the left at the bottom of the page opposite. Sleeves became more and more excessive, longer and looser. Some were cut at the elbow or shoulder to allow them to hang loose, or to be tucked into the belt or girdle at the side and display the sleeve of the doublet or jerkin worn underneath.

Striped tights or hose, still worn a great deal on the Continent, were also frequently seen in England, but the mode of stocks with legs made from different coloured materials was seldom adopted on this side of the Channel.

Men's hair was still worn long, though usually cut in the manner of a longish " bob " in preference to the shoulder-length curls seen at the opening of the century.

1510—1520 (*continued*)

While a number of varied examples of women's apparel naturally appear in these pages, it should be understood that the nun-like head-dress and gown were still the most generally worn. The lady in black on the opposite page is, perhaps, the most typical Englishwoman. The rather exaggerated figure at the top right-hand corner is more representative of the Flemish or German style often seen in England at this time. The extravagant modes of slashing and tying with "points" were general in most European countries.

The unfortunate children of the sixteenth century were dressed as exact replicas of their parents, but this does not seem to have hindered them from playing such games as hoops, leap-frog, stool ball, and many others equally active. Babies were all swaddled or swathed until they reached the age of six months or more, the idea being that the legs and arms must necessarily grow straight if tied in that position. There is small wonder that infant mortality was so excessive; the heat inside these swathings must have been unbearable during the summer months, and should the mother or nurse bind them too tight, the miserable child was doomed to deformity of the shoulders and thorax.

1510—1520 (*continued*)

The woman on the right at the bottom of the preceding page is wearing the gable head-dress with its lappets folded back to show the long side-pieces of the coif worn underneath. Hairdressing with this form of head-dress now assumes a mode of its own: either the hair was parted in the centre and the front part bound with ribbon and recrossed on the forehead, or—perhaps when the hair was thin or short—the front hair was encased in rolls of striped silk or cotton and arranged in a similar manner. The hair at the back was worn loose under the veil. Occasionally we find examples of the striped pad pushed farther back on the head and showing the centre parting of the hair in front, as may be seen among the group of heads on page 31.

The large velvet hats, slashed and decorated with gems and feathers, were not of English origin, but were brought over from Germany, France, and Spain. Several leading English ladies of the Court favoured these more masculine fashions. Anne Boleyn was rarely painted in anything nun-like, but her known portraits represent quite a valuable collection of rather masculine hats. The coif and the circlet of gold and gems with a short veil behind appeared about 1503, and seem to have remained in favour until supplanted by the Tudor cap made so popular by Mary Queen of Scots.

1520—1530

A NOTICEABLE change in the cut of the under-garment occurred about the 'twenties of this century. The neck-line gradually rose until it took the form of a minute frill—the first small beginning of the ruff to come. This fashion was more general for the man, women still preferring an open neck in most cases, although there are many examples of the high-necked shift.

Heavily embroidered materials gained brilliance by the addition of sewn pearls and beads and other semi-precious and precious stones. In the frontispiece is shown the first example of the treble sleeve, a fashion rigidly adhered to whenever the bell-shaped sleeve to the gown was worn. This consisted of a detachable short sleeve or cuff of a stiff embroidered material—in its early stages frequently striped; worn over the lawn or cambric under-garment, and joined by "points," thus showing the under-sleeve, which was pulled out in puffs. This large cuff finished a few inches above the elbow, and, as the fashion progressed, became larger, until it formed a complete half-circle of stiff material folded and fastened in the manner described.

About 1525 the woman's skirt, which previously had been a complete affair, was cut up the front to form an inverted V, which disclosed a sumptuous embroidered petticoat, usually of contrasting colours to the gown or kirtle. A tendency to stiffen the petticoats and make the skirt stand away from the body was first noticeable about this date. The train also had practically disappeared from general use by about 1520, although it was still worn by ladies of the Court and for all ceremonious occasions; the train of this period was not the separate hanging train as we know it to-day, but the trailing point which was a feature of all gowns worn during the first twenty years of the sixteenth century.

The figure on the left at the bottom of the opposite page is an exceedingly interesting example of German fashions, a striking contrast to the very English lady facing her. There are few remaining examples of such pleated skirts, probably the weight of them was too much for the majority of women to bear, and the mode could not have existed for more than a very few years. It is, however amusing to note the amazing similarity between this figure and those of fashion plates of about one hundred years ago, between 1825–30. Fashions are for ever changing—but never advancing.

1520—1530 (*continued*)

Of trunk-hose, the breeches are called " upper-stocks," and " nether-stocks " is the name for the stocking-like part covering the foot, calf, and frequently the thigh. Practically throughout the century these were joined together to form one complete garment. The second man on the previous page is wearing one of the earliest pairs of " paned " upper-stocks, an effect achieved by slashing in even strips, or more rarely by means of separate ribbon-like attachments of embroidery. It will be noticed that as the century advanced they became looser and were stuffed out to their fullest capacity. This same man is also ornamented with *picadils*, the folded and cut material visible on the shoulders, wrists, and where the upper and nether stocks are joined. This exceedingly popular form of decoration was used by both sexes, and several examples, especially as a shoulder and neck decoration, will be found in the ensuing pages.

Shoes, which previously had been somewhat round-toed, developed into the well-known square, padded, and slashed shape in which Henry VIII was wont to be depicted. Sometimes these were ridiculously exaggerated, even to eight or nine inches width at the toe, with tufts of coloured lining pulled out through the slashes. They were tied at the ankle with a thin leather lace, which came from behind the heel of the shoe, not from the instep. On the page facing is an example of loose *panes* tied just above the knee to form yet a second bulge. At this early period, however, little or no stuffing was worn, merely a loose lining which could be drawn out through the panes if the wearer so desired.

1520—1530 (*continued*)

With the rise of the neck of the doublet and jerkin a small collar sometimes appeared, though this fashion seems to have been more military than civil until about 1535, when it became general.

The head-dresses illustrated here need little or no explanation. The gable at the bottom has the lappets folded and the veil split and laid back over the head-dress. The man next to this is wearing an exaggerated form of the traditional cap, and the loose, open pleats on his gown are clearly seen. The top left-hand figure is taken from a portrait of Anne Boleyn, and the gewgaw that hangs from the ridiculous cap is a typical addition.

It is impossible to over-emphasize the general extravagance of ornament among the wealthy. The amazing richness of embroidery, and the dazzling addition of jewels, could not conceivably be illustrated in a much larger book than this. If it be borne in mind that practically every square inch of the garments reproduced in these pages was ornamented, slashed, embroidered, and bejewelled, that magnificent pearls, jewels, and precious stones adorned practically every finger, trimmed every head-dress, decorated every neck, and were woven into every garment, then it may be possible to gain some idea of the extravagant splendour of a Court in the reign of Henry VIII. At no later period in the history of our country has the Court wallowed in so much gold and silver and priceless materials. And probably at no time have the poor been so squalidly housed and filthily garbed as they were during this amazing reign.

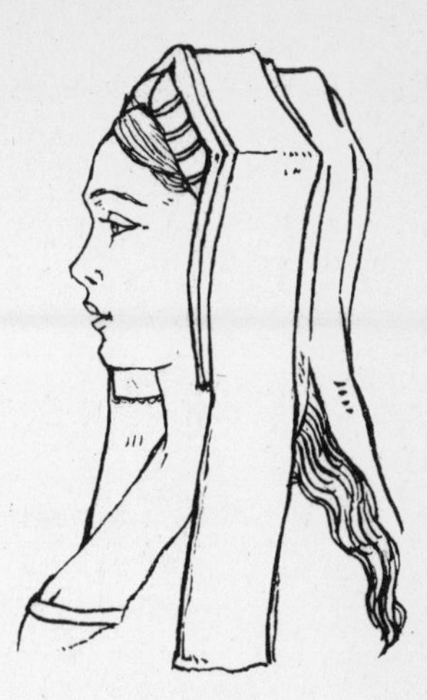

1530—1540

THE female example on the facing page is not, strictly speaking, the most typical of the period 1530–1540. It is, indeed, the German type of gown and hat adopted in England during the 'thirties, and rarely seen later than 1534. However, I have chosen it in this instance to give the reader some idea of the detail in design which I have already mentioned. Spot patterns and interchange designs were very popular, and the acanthus leaf figured extensively in all floral designs. The lady's gown or kirtle is of purple velvet, richly worked with silver thread; the lower part of the sleeve is white cloth-of-tissue with a traced design in gold. Under this she wears a pleated petticoat of yellow damask. The neck of the gown is heavily set with stones, and her belt and necklet are both of gold, with rubies and pearls inset. Her hat is of black velvet, also bravely adorned with many precious stones.

The gentleman beside her is a typical example of the fashionable Englishman of the late 'thirties. From now on a new item of men's clothing takes shape in the form of a waistcoat. The doublet is cut low to reveal the splendour of this beautifully embroidered and pearled garment. The latter in its turn is slashed to show off the fine lawn or satin shirt beneath. In this example the sleeves are made of the same material and design as the waistcoat, the doublet being sleeveless. The doublet is made of black velvet and decorated with bands of crewel-work, as is the skirt or base, which is split in front, showing the cod-piece, a feature of men's apparel until the 'eighties. The stocks are made of velvet, black at the top, and blue nether-stocks. Over all is the jerkin of light blue broadcloth lined with miniver; the elbow-length sleeves are slashed and show the fur linings.

1530—1540 (*continued*)

Let us for a moment imagine ourselves transported in time over just four hundred years back to the scenes of Anne Boleyn's coronation. From the Tower to the Temple the city is alive with excitement. Cheapside, Cornhill, and Grace Street are marvellously decorated with gold and silver cloth and rich velvet hangings. The constables of the City, richly clad in velvet and silk, hold great staves in their hands to keep back the seething crowd of would-be spectators. From every gaily-trapped window excited and curious heads crane to get a glimpse of the new Queen.

Amid yells of applause and welcoming cheers the procession winds its way through the narrow, overcrowded streets. Foremost rides the Lord Mayor, splendid in his crimson velvet gown lined and trimmed with fur, his large gold chain flashing impressively in the sunlight. He is followed by footmen in white and red damask, then by twelve mounted Frenchmen clothed in blue velvet with blue and yellow sleeves, their horses' trappings a blue sarsenet ground with white crosses. Then proceeds a stately assortment of Knights, Squires, Judges, Gentlemen, Abbots, Barons, Bishops, Earls, and Marquises, these all gowned in scarlet or crimson. The Knights Commanders of the Bath wear gorgeous violet velvet, with hoods embroidered in gold and silver and " purled " with miniver!

Then at last, as we grow dizzy with so brilliant a spectacle, the Queen appears, a striking figure in white amongst such a riot of colour. Her litter of white cloth of gold is borne by two palfries in white damask. Her kirtle is of white cloth of tissue, her mantle of the same, wonderfully furred with ermine; down her back hangs her fair hair, and on her head is a coif with a circlet about it full of rich and rare stones. And carried by four knights is the canopy of cloth of gold with gilt staves to shield her from the sun.

1530—1540 (*continued*)

Behind the Queen ride the Lord Chancellor and the Masters of the Horse; then come the ladies of the Court, all in scarlet velvet turned up with gold and tissue, their horses in magnificent trappings of cloth-of-gold. And, last of all, the gentlewomen of the Court are drawn in chariots of cloth-of-gold and clothed in scarlet and crimson. The procession passes, and a motley collection of shopkeepers, marketers, children, beggars, and sightseers crowd across the road, cheering. Such is the indelible picture that is left us by a contemporary historian. There are a thousand and one equally interesting details, especially of the feast: the amazing dishes they ate, the incredible quantity of wines and ales consumed, how Anne sat at the head of an immense table—her ladies to the left, gentlemen to the right—and was served with twenty-six dishes to each course.

This page of drawings and the one preceding it give various examples of the gradually changing style; the high neck for the shirt was practically always worn, and was finished with a *partlet strip*, or upstanding separate collar, which perhaps was the first version of the starched atrocity worn by men of to-day. A tiny shoulder-cape of velvet or cloth was often worn by ladies at this time, and a high-necked yoke of some material contrasting in colour with the gown seems to have been very popular until the 'fifties. Skirts were gradually becoming fuller and fuller, the hems just touching the ground all round.

1530—1540 (*continued*)

Several different types of caps were worn indoors by matrons and by domestics, and many varieties of the coif developed eventually into the upstanding semicircular head-dress, of which the top right-hand illustration is an example. This was so heavy with jewels and ornaments that it had to be tied under the chin with a narrow white cord to stop it sliding down the back of the wearer's head.

From about 1535 men's caps began to be worn with the brim down, instead of turned up as had previously been the case. The same style of cap was adopted by many ladies and worn over the coif. Between the years 1530 and 1540 a short bowl-like cut of the hair was introduced for men—a transition stage between the "bob" and the short hair fashionable for half a century from about 1545; an instance of this style appears on the next page, worn by the boy in blue. Ear-pieces, cut to cover the ears and nape of the neck, were apparently quite a regular addition to many caps, both for men and women. Sometimes a close velvet cap with ear-flaps and a cord under the chin was worn, this seems to have been called a "night cap," though whether it was worn day and night is impossible to say.

1540—1550

HERE is an example of the bell-skirt without folds, cut across the weave of the material to give the skirt the flared effect at the hem. In its earliest stages it is doubtful whether any actual wire structure was worn; the full, creaseless effect was probably obtained by padding at the hip and by a stiffened hem, combined with the addition of numerous petticoats. However, with the introduction of the Spanish *vertingale* about fifteen or twenty years later, there appears little or no difference in the outline except, perhaps, for an added width of hem.

There was a general tendency to tightness of contour about 1540. The sleeves, for instance, previously soft and malleable, became stiff and somewhat bulky, owing to a certain extent to the increased embroidery on the surface of the materials, and also to the craze for bombasting or stiffening which was just beginning to be noticeable. High leather corsets were generally worn by ladies of fashion, and these were responsible for the curious bolster-like effect so evident in Holbein's portraits.

A dress with a yoke nearly always seems to have had a high stand-up collar open in front. There are also a few examples of the yoked dress finishing with a minute ruff. In the example opposite the yoke is made of fur, but instances of this are rare.

The bonnet-like cap worn by the small boy is certainly amusing and not wholly devoid of charm; it was apparently worn solely by children and elderly men. The other child has his jerkin guarded with the fashionable narrow black bands.

1540—1550 (*continued*)

It is exceedingly difficult to find contemporary examples of the costume of serving men and women of this period—no doubt few, if any, ever had the opportunity of sitting for their portraits. An excellent example, however, is reproduced in each of the drawings opposite. The woman's dress is particularly interesting, and shows us that pleated petticoats were in general use; the little striped cap is of an unusual shape, in fact I have been unable to find more than three or four similar examples, and one of these was made of fur. The idea of fastening the skirt to the belt was probably to protect it from getting unnecessarily spotted in front, for although the effect obtained is in itself exceedingly becoming, it is doubtful whether such was the chief consideration.

Two interesting points to note in the male figure at the top are, firstly, the *mock coat*, a cloak with sleeves entirely for ornamentation; and, secondly, the upper stocks or breeches which, as is typical in these garments' early stages, have a tight-fitting hip-yoke, the *panes* only beginning from the top of the leg, and reaching half-way down the thigh. In this instance they are joined slantwise. The huge square shoulders, padded and bombasted, reached their height of absurdity during this decade, and slowly sank back to a more normal form. At the close of Henry VIII's reign (he died in 1547) shoes began to be made with leather or velvet, covering the instep, and with an inch or so of added protection for the heel. The toes, still squarish, were less exaggerated, and slashing was made in some instances both sideways and upwards. With the death of the King fashions seemed suddenly to mark time, and until the accession of Elizabeth in 1558 very little change took place.

1540—1550 (*continued*)

Bodices or stomachers of gowns gradually assumed a point in front, in preference to the straight line at the waist. About 1545, and for some five years later, they were fastened down the front, the opening being faced with jewels or embroidery and stiffened with wooden busks.

Little girls were forcibly corsetted at a ridiculously early age, and quite probably this was the cause of the deformed shoulders of so many women mentioned by contemporary historians, both at this date and later in the century. It certainly seems impossible, to our modern minds, that any child's bones could develop in a normal manner when hampered with corsets which not only reached from armpits to hips, but were made of leather, wood, or even metal. But these ancestors of ours must have been amazingly hardy. They lived and died surrounded by such an odd mixture of revolting cruelty, dirt, and disease on the one hand, and on the other sumptuous wealth, splendour, and bravery seemingly out of all perspective. Their streets were so foul with drainage and rubbish that clogs, or *chopins*, had to be worn to lift their feet above the filth. Yet their damp and draughty halls were decorated with priceless tapestries, furnished with wonderful hand-carved furniture, and hung with beautiful damasks ; their tables were set with gold and silver cups and platters, and their kitchens richly and plentifully supplied with every conceivable variety of meat, fish, and fowl.

1540—1550 (*continued*)

These sixteenth-century Englishmen were compounded of paradox. They could apparently witness, merely as interested spectators, an acquaintance being hanged, drawn, and quartered. They could set out in small ships to discover new worlds and face unknown dangers. And yet they were terrified of witchcraft, and wore charms and amulets to avert the evil eye, and consulted oracles, and indulged in love-potions in all seriousness. They grumbled and worried over the problem of traffic-control in the City, and over the price of meat when it rose from three-farthings a pound to one penny. At times they were so strangely like ourselves, and at times such worlds apart. Their persons reflected these extremes, especially in the lack of fastidiousness beneath gorgeous exteriors. Baths were considered unnecessary and unhealthy, fresh air was bad for the lungs, sweet scents were held by most to be evil—cloying the senses and therefore inviting the devil. Small wonder that when Henry walked abroad he carried in his hand "an Orange whereof the substance had been taken out and filled up with a sponge full of vinegar and other confections against the Pestilent Ayres, the which he most commonly held to his nose in a press."

Men's caps became gradually larger in the crown until crown and brim were almost the same width; the crown was higher, too, than formerly, and somewhat stiffer. About 1550, ruffles came into being. At first, however, they were devoid of starch, which was not discovered until some ten years later; they were made of holland or lawn and, as will be seen in the illustration, somewhat irregular in form. The tiny ruffle at the top of the *partlet* strip was quite general for both sexes.

1550—1560

DURING this decade the people of England were under three successive sovereigns, each totally different in character and qualities, and their changing influences reacted noticeably upon the style and cut of clothes, even if there was no great variety in costume until after Mary's death.

The first three years, under the youthful Edward VI, saw little or no change. The boy was delicate, and the country seemed to stand still, waiting to see what would happen next. But with the accession of Mary, and the introduction of a Spanish prince as king, fashions began to change. Various Spanish styles were brought into the country, the chief of them the *vertingale*, or farthingale, a somewhat similar affair to the crinoline of the nineteenth century. An amazing variety of new head-dresses and caps supplanted the rather hackneyed coif-and-circlet and the gable head-dress, and for men a hat took the place of the flat cap in many instances. Throughout her reign Mary herself clung tenaciously to the old styles, and innovations were certainly not adopted with any display of interest on her part; the Court, therefore, was practically compelled to adhere to the high-waisted, bell-sleeved gowns, and the coif or caul with the circlet. The caul head-dress with the circlet disappeared at the end of Mary's reign, and probably it was cast aside with a sigh of relief. Most certainly it was exceedingly awkward and heavy to carry, and we read of Mary's coronation that "she wore . . . on her head a caule of cloth of tinsel beset with pearl and stone, and above the same a round circlet of gold beset so richly with precious stones that the value thereof was infinite. The same caule and circlet being so massive and ponderous that she was fayne to bear up her head with her hand." She must have had a ghastly headache after the twelve-hour ceremony.

1550—1560 (*continued*)

In the year 1556 the Ambassador of the Emperor of Russia came to England to pay his respects to Mary and Philip, and there is an interesting list of the gifts showered upon him to take back to the Emperor, which reflects the amazing value set on fine raiment:

"First, two rich pieces of cloth of tissue.
Item, one fine piece of scarlet.
Item, one fine violet in graine.
Item, one azure cloth.
Item, a notable paire of brigandine, with a murian covered with crimson velvet, and gilt nails."

A personal gift to the Ambassador from the Queen included:

"One rich piece of cloth of tissue, a piece of cloth of gold, another piece of cloth of golde raised with crimson velvet, a piece of crimson velvet in graine, a piece of damask purpled, a piece of purple velvet and a piece of crimson damask."

So overjoyed with this wonderful gift was the Emperor that he promptly returned the compliment by having large quantities of rare furs and live animals shipped to the Queen of England. History unfortunately does not state whether these fine beasts were immediately slaughtered for their magnificent fur, or if they were kept as royal pets.

The five years of Mary's reign were among the cruelest and most cold-blooded in our history, yet we find details of these polite international exchanges of pieces of cloth described at far greater length than any of the epoch-making slaughters or executions, possibly because the latter were too numerous and commonplace to be commented upon.

1550—1560 (*continued*)

The bell-shaped sleeve totally disappeared with the accession of Elizabeth in 1558. The new style favoured a tight-fitting sleeve with a large "puff" at the shoulder and a tiny frill or ruffle at the wrist. This puff was frequently quite separate, or it might belong to the gown and the sleeve itself be separate. The new arrangement was equally popular for men's wear. The full bombasted and slashed sleeves never quite lost favour throughout this reign; about the year 1590, indeed, they became even more popular than at any previous date.

Mantles, or *surcotes*, with short puff sleeves were worn, even indoors at times, their fullness increasing at the hem to give an idea of even folds from top to bottom. Many examples of these delightfully formal garments may be seen upon the effigies on contemporary tombs; but in such instances it is quite impossible, owing to the absurd effect of any but the simplest drapery on a recumbent figure, to obtain any idea of the Spanish *vertingale* or full-bottomed skirt which was undoubtedly worn at that time.

Probably the reason for so many changes in fashion about 1558–1600 was that Elizabeth was a comparatively bright young person, who had been imprisoned and suppressed for many years. The effect of sudden access to practically unlimited wealth and freedom and power was that she promptly stocked her wardrobe with all the gowns she desired. We certainly know that she was fond of clothes—at one time in her life at least she possessed three thousand dresses at once, or so historians tell us. In fact, Richmond Palace was called the Queen's wardrobe, being practically filled with her gowns that were not in use.

1550—1560 (*continued*)

With the introduction of new styles of head-dress the centre parting became less general. The hair was brushed back from the forehead rather loosely to make a slight puff round the face, and later was padded on either side so that it might fill the curve of the cap, as may be seen on the page facing. The heart-shaped cap, commonly associated with Mary Queen of Scots, became amazingly fashionable and continued in fashion with many slight alterations until caps ceased to be worn. They were at first worn over a small embroidered cap, as seen at the top of the previous page.

Heavily embroidered and jewelled bands of material seem to have been the most popular method of decoration for most garments, and of course *picadils* were still as popular. Bone-lace was also used a great deal, both as a trimming and as a hat-band for men. Heavy gold neck-chains were not as popular as the narrow cord or ribbon, with a locket attached; the locket either carried a portrait of a lover, some precious stone, or a tiny miniature. Women wore similar cords tied round their waists, and on these a rosary was sometimes worn. Ear-rings were very popular for both sexes, the gallant often preferring to wear only one. Small ruffles were worn by practically everyone, for the huge turn-down collar became more popular in the 'sixties.

1560—1570

SOME account of the development of trunk-hose has already been given, but this example conveys a better idea of their actual structure than any written explanation. In surviving contemporary specimens it is not until those of the 'sixties that we can see with any clearness how these trunk-hose were composed; but when the jerkin no longer covers the doublet several excellent examples are forthcoming. Although the *panes* are clearly shown in the costume illustrated here, it should be explained that the "drawings-out" were in most cases definitely fuller than these. Sometimes as many as a dozen yards of material were used in the stuffing of one pair, and if this was particularly fine it was pulled out several inches beyond the *panes*.

From about 1565 breeches began to assume gigantic proportions, and, although the cut seems to have varied, the common practice was to stuff them with bran, wool, hair, rags, or anything else that might be at hand. Soldiers found them particularly useful for storing loot. So absurdly large did they become that a scaffold was erected in the Houses of Parliament "for those to sit on who used the wearing of great breeches stuffed with hair like wool sacks." Apparently it was impossible to sit with any degree of comfort on an ordinary chair. What method was adopted in the home to make seating possible it is difficult to say; there are no records of chairs differing in structure, in fact existing examples of Elizabethan furniture show us that few chairs were without arms.

1560—1570 (*continued*)

In the year 1564 starch was introduced into England by a certain Mistress Dingham Vander Plasse. So great was the demand for education in starching that she started a school of instruction in the composition of starch, and charged several pounds for imparting this knowledge to young ladies of rank. The problem of laundering was solved, and ruffles began to grow enormously in size. But this knowledge took several years to filter down through the masses, and not until the 'seventies was the large "ruff" worn by everyone. There are several existing prints representing the laundering and forming of ruffs during the 'seventies and 'eighties of the sixteenth century.

Starch in its earliest days was tinted yellow, so that the first big ruffles were invariably creamy in colour. The fashion died, however, when a certain notorious Mrs. Turner was hanged at Tyburn in one of these yellow ruffles. After this gruesome episode the modish shade turned from yellow to blue, probably very little different in its palest tints from the starch we use to-day. Frequently the ruff was untied in front to give a little more air and freedom to the wearer, for it is difficult to imagine any form of neck-wear more uncomfortable than a closed ruff. Large upstanding collars were worn by women who did not favour the ruffle, and the turned-down collar already mentioned was worn by men. The neck was not visible again until the 'nineties of the century, but there are numerous instances of a gown itself finishing with a low, square line at the shoulders so that a considerable expanse of bare chest was visible under the ruffle and above the gown.

1560—1570 (*continued*)

During the year 1565 the problem of unemployment in cloth-manufacturing towns became chronic, because so many imported silks and velvets were used that there was little or no demand for the woollens and cottons manufactured in England. An appeal was made to the Queen, who issued a proclamation forbidding any further importation of materials from the Continent, and further ordering that every man should wear a woollen cap unless he had an income of over forty pounds a year. Whether these official commands made any impression on the people is difficult to say, but it is certain that the effect, if any, was not lasting, because garments, instead of losing brilliance, seem to have become even more rich and ornate than before. And the woollen cap was not nearly as popular as the velvet one, or as the more fashionable hat. If the Queen had followed up her proclamation by herself appearing in some woollen or cotton gown instead of the exaggerated foreign styles she invariably adopted, the royal decrees might have been more effective.

The first figure on the opposite page is wearing an excellent example of the Spanish *vertingale* or farthingale, and the general use of small slashes and picadils is shown. It is difficult to exaggerate the importance attached to details at this period : the garments illustrated here may appear comparatively simple, but in reality they were crowded with minute designs, lace, embroidery, guards and gold *aglets* (small eyelet holes for the " points ").

1560—1570 (*continued*)

A little may be said here about the wearing of beards in the Sixteenth Century. For the first twenty years of the period men were clean-shaven. Henry VIII, however, started to grow a beard at about the age of twenty-three, and a few years afterwards the mode became popular among the nobility. By 1545 the fashion had spread, and beards were far more prevalent than clean-shaven faces. The pointed beard and small pointed moustache first came into vogue during the 'fifties, probably another introduction from Spain by Philip. The beard became gradually smaller and neater until the 'nineties, and by about 1600 had assumed the size and shape of a small triangular postage-stamp stuck in the middle of the chin. Tiny moustaches with no beard were also fashionable from about 1570 to the end of the century.

The two upper head-dresses on opposite page are interesting in that they represent some of the amusing transitional stages between head-dresses and hats, the one on the right being distinctly reminiscent of the policeman's helmet of to-day. Men's hats with a large brim and a shallow crown were not worn for more than a few years in this decade; they were followed by a craze for high crowns, but became popular again during the late 'eighties. Caps at this time had little or no brim, but a band of lace, embroidery, or jewels was usually worn as a form of decoration.

1570—1580

WITH the 'seventies came several entirely new fashions for men. The doublet began to develop a sort of padded and stiffened point in front, whence it was commonly known as the " peascod-belly " doublet, of which one of the earliest examples is illustrated here; this fashion became ridiculously exaggerated during the 'eighties. The *mandilion* was almost as popular as the cloak; it was a short, full coat or jerkin with hanging sleeves, the sides often split to show the doublet underneath. Cloaks were most fashionable, short, barely reaching to the hips, and sometimes worn swathed round in the Venetian style, as may be seen on the left-hand figure at the foot of the next page. Shoulder-padding was general, and " wings " were added to accentuate the width of the doublet.

Short stockings called boot-hose were worn under the boot to save the hose from unnecessary friction; similar in shape to the golf-stocking of to-day, they were made of rich materials and beautifully embroidered. Venetians, a species of knee-breeches, bombasted, quilted, and padded, came into vogue about 1572. These usually reached just to the knee, and were either tied with a wide garter or finished with a small frill or band. Whenever trunk-hose were worn they were so abbreviated as barely to cover the buttocks, and as the peascod doublet became more exaggerated the trunks developed into a mere small roll a few inches deep, sometimes hardly visible under the huge doublet in front. It should be remembered here that after about 1550 the term " upper-stocks " was dropped in favour of the more general " trunk-hose," so that in describing hose the roll or pumpkin-like top was usually called " trunk-hose," and the leg covering itself termed " nether-stocks."

1570—1580 (*continued*)

About six or seven years after the introduction of " Venetians," yet another new style came into being—trunk-hose with canions. A loose stocking-like appendage was attached to the padded trunks and reached just below the knee; the nether-stocks were separate and drew up like a stocking over the canions, fastening with a garter either just above or below the knee. One of the earliest examples of this style is to be seen on the lower left-hand figure on the opposite page. An interesting variation of the trunk-hose, especially amusing for its plus-fours appearance, is worn by the upper left-hand figure. This variation was, however, of German or Swiss origin, and not frequently seen in England. When this style was worn the padding was all of loose material, not bombast, and the drawings-out through the panes were sometimes so liberal that the panes themselves were practically invisible.

Silks, velvets, satins, damasks, sarcenet, taffeta, and châlet were the most popular materials. Although all these were imported, the old trouble of unemployment in manufacturing towns seems by this time to have been to some degree avoided by the large export trade in wools, kerseys, dozens, penistone cottons, fustians, buffins, cameleons, linsey-woolsey, and many other interesting materials. All these apparently were not suitable foundations for the exquisite tailoring and abundant embroidery lavished on practically all English garments at this time.

About this time Elizabeth was presented with a pair of silk stockings woven by one of her ladies, and after wearing these she decided to dispense with any other form of hose. Whether she was actually the first person in England to wear hand-knitted stockings it is difficult to say—there are records of Edward VII having a pair of silk hose given him, and apparently they were hand-knitted. However, after the 'sixties silk nether-stocks became exceedingly fashionable in spite of the fact that as much as five pounds was paid for a single pair.

1570—1580 (*continued*)

Women's clothes also became more exaggerated in style. One particularly new garment was the transparent cobweb lawn cloak or veil, with a large, upstanding, heart-shaped collar, in some cases closely resembling a hood. These cloaks or veils often reached to the ground, and were decorated with a tiny edge of lace.

Towards the end of this decade came the French *vertingale* or farthingale. This was vastly different from the Spanish vertingale in that the contour, instead of being cone-shaped, was more like that of a drum with the upper rim tilted down in the front. This effect was obtained with the help of a large whalebone frame of cart-wheel shape fitted to the hips and tipped up at the back by shortening the spoke-like attachments. The skirt worn over this was exceedingly full, and shorter than any other form of dress at this period. Sometimes a similar effect was obtained by the wearing of a bolster-like padding tied round the waist. There were many variations of this fashion: sometimes a short, loosely gathered basque was worn over the skirt finishing at the hoop, and later an immense ruffle, similar to the ones worn about the neck, was attached to the waist and reached out to the edge of the drum. The Spanish farthingale did not lose its popularity with the introduction of the French, and in some contemporary paintings we can see clearly that the skirt was sometimes held out by means of a single hoop at the hem and a little padding at the waist.

1570—1580 (*continued*)

Hats now began to assume a jaunty and, to us, an amusing aspect. Beaver—alluded to as a curious kind of hair—was quite popular by about 1578. Sarcenet, wool, taffeta, and velvet were all used in the making of hats. Ladies often wore them over a tight-fitting cap. The hat-band was a specially valuable possession, as this was frequently adorned with precious stones and pearls.

Contemporary moralists wrote scathingly of the absurdities of fashion, and particularly of the wickedness of using cosmetics. One such writer took it upon himself to deliver this awful warning: "Those which paint or colour themselves in this world otherwise than God hath made them, let them feare lest when the daie of judgement commeth the Lorde will not knowe them for his creatures."

Writers of this period seem to have been divided into two definite classes: Those who indulged in every possible extravagance and excuse for indecency in their literary efforts, and stern moralists who, in their somewhat wild efforts to crush extravagance, rigorously damned everything pertaining to beauty, cleanliness, fastidiousness, or general improvements. The former upheld the gaiety and brilliance of Court life, the feasting, drinking, and general debauchery, and they give us a fairly accurate account of the life of any young gallant who was not afraid to sow sufficient wild-oats to drive him out of his town, or even out of the country, for a few years.

1580—1590

THE peascod doublet reached the height, or depth, of absurdity during these ten years; after about 1590 few exaggerated styles were to be seen. Not only were these doublets exceedingly hot and bulky for the unfortunate wearer, but he experienced great difficulty in any endeavour to stoop. So stuffed, bombasted, and quilted did they become that the points actually reached some eight or nine inches below the belt. The idea of the unitiated appears to have been that these doublets were designed especially to further "gourmandie and gluttonie." As eating and drinking was one of the chief pastimes during the latter part of the century, there may have been some truth in so sweeping an assertion, and consideration of the figures illustrated on the next page makes it easy to sympathize with this view. When we read of the amazing dishes of capons, larks, sparrows, roast oxen, boars' heads, and innumerable pies—including, of course, the then rare delicacy, "potato pyes"—that were habitually consumed at one sitting, it is hard to avoid believing that some sort of camouflage for undue stoutness was necessary.

The Anatomie of Abuses suggests that the exaggerated fashions worn at this time were not altogether approved, even by their wearers: "For moste of our new-fangled fashions dooe thei not rather deforme us than adorne us, disguise us than become us, makyng us rather semble savage Beastes and sterne monsters than continent sober christians?" Probably this reasonable point of view accounts for the comparatively short popularity of the peascod belly in this country. Nevertheless it is the period immortalized by Punch and Judy, for even to-day Punch may be seen with his ruffle and peascod doublet.

1580—1590 (*continued*)

Women started to frizz and crimp their hair during the 'eighties, and, as the "puffed" effect grew in favour, wire frames were devised to support their frizzed and curled locks. "Wreaths" and "borders" were arranged across the top of the head from ear to ear; these were sometimes imitation flowers, or even precious stones set in a gold or silver framework. Wigs and added pieces of hair became popular, and dyes were used so extensively that a lady of fashion was rarely seen at two succeeding functions with her hair the same shade. As additional decorations, rings, beads, pearls, precious stones, and other gewgaws were fixed among the curls in a manner called enchanting by contemporaries. The hair apparently became a nesting-place for any extra piece of jewellery that could not be affixed elsewhere.

Elizabeth herself specialized in wigs, red and a sort of saffron colour being her two favourite shades. Some fashionable ladies not blessed with such an abundance of hair as their more fortunate sisters, and probably unwilling to go to the expense of buying wigs, bribed peasant women and children to part with their locks for a few pence, and thus added to their inadequate supply of crowning glory. The hair being eventually arranged or "laid out" to the wearer's satisfaction, a large velvet or beaver hat was perched on the front or side of the head; these hats were similar to those worn by men and invariably had a feather worn in the hat-band.

1580—1590 (*continued*)

It will be noticed that whenever the French farthingale was worn a stiff V-shaped stomacher invariably accompanied it. This was worn at a slight angle to the body, fitting at the breast and gradually sloping outwards, till the base of the V rested on the tilted front of the farthingale. In several portraits of the time the hand is hidden behind this, which means that in some cases the stomacher must have been worn loose. Tight-lacing was exceedingly prevalent, and there are records that " since busks came in request horn is scarce." Girls endeavoured to make their waists so small that they could span them with their hands. This wasp-waist outline was augmented by the use, above and below the corset, of " little bolsters or pillows for to seem more fat and comely." The shoulders were padded and the sleeves bombasted in violent contrast to the small waist.

Ruffles during the 'eighties became so large and unwieldy that an under-prop was devised to lift them up. Sometimes the ruffle was pinned to the ears; in other instances it fell down over the shoulders.

Cork-soled shoes called *pinsnets* and *pantoffles* were worn; these had a heel about an inch or an inch and a half high, and their wearers had great difficulty in managing to walk with them. So uncomfortable were they that frequently men's legs swelled from wearing them. Every possible colour and material was used in the making of these shoes.

Hose made from jersey, worsted, crewell, yarn, thread, and of course the most fashionable silk, were dyed as many different colours as the shoes. An interesting list of fashionable shades includes " russet, saffron, black, white, red, grene, yellowe, watchet, blew and pink." Scabbards and sheaths were made from velvet and even embroidered linen.

1580—1590 (*continued*)

Ladies at this time wore beautifully embroidered and scented gloves and shoes or " pumps " made of cheverill, silk, or velvet. When walking abroad they carried black velvet masks to shield their complexions from the sun, or to disguise them from undesirable acquaintances. Fans with silver handles were very popular, and practically every woman carried a small hand-mirror either attached to her girdle or hanging on a cord about her neck. These looking-glasses were rudely alluded to as " Devil's Spectacles " by contemporary moralists—" And good reason, else how could they see the devil in themselves ? "

Apparently rather childish and demure mannerisms, and a craze for " baby-talk," were adopted by the most fashionable ladies. These must have seemed more than a little absurd, and in violent contrast to their stiff, bombasted appearances—and, by all accounts, their ultra-sophisticated and immoral behaviour. Let it be said at once that at least Elizabeth did not set the vogue for " baby-talk " ; her vocabulary would probably shock even the broadest-minded of men of to-day. Shakespeare does not give the impression that a mincing of words was the general trend of the time, and his works are amazingly discreet compared with others written at the same period. Men were certainly somewhat coarse in their behaviour, even if effeminate in their apparel : spitting, tobacco-chewing, and tooth-picking were all reckoned elegant accomplishments.

1590—1600

THE century ends in a wild orgy of extravagance. Even the country people, previously content with their russet smocks and *mockados*, now emulated their superiors in every conceivable manner and blossomed out in silks and satins whenever in any way possible, selling their last cow or pig to buy a pair of fine silk hose to excite the envy of their less well-apparelled neighbours. Clothes seem to have become the principal consideration in life, and so many and varied were the styles for men that the fop or gallant could hardly have one suit completed before it was out of fashion. In Ben Jonson's *Everyman out of his Humour*, the young collegiate tries desperately to keep pace with the latest demands of fashion, and in consequence gets head-over-heels in debt, because as fast as his tailor turns out one style he sees another which is newer and therefore more desirable. The fashionable lady is seen vividly and entertainingly through the eyes of a contemporary poet :

> . . . Wear curled Periwigs and chalk their faces
> And still are gazing in their pocket glasses.
> Tyred with pinned ruffles, fans and partlet-strips
> With Buskes and Vertingales about their hips.
> And tread on Corked Stilts at pris'nor's pace,
> And make their napkin for their spitting place.

The whole century was such a comical mixture of polished indecency and crude exquisiteness that it is only after reading dozens of contemporary volumes that we can hope to obtain even a glimmering understanding of these ancestors of ours. Doubtless an Elizabethan gentleman landed suddenly amongst us to-day would consider our modes and manners equally inconsistent and amusing.

The magnificent costume illustrated here provides an interesting example of sixteenth-century design. Some time during the 'eighties a fashion for depicting scenes, animals, birds, fishes, or anything which might be a typical emblem of the wearer, had been adopted as a motif for design. This particular petticoat—drawn from a garment belonging to Elizabeth—is probably intended to show some of the beasts, flowers, fish, and fowl to be found in her dominions, and the foreign waters explored by her sea captains. There is also an existing portrait of Sir Francis Drake, in the National Portrait Gallery, apparently painted soon after his circumnavigation, which clearly shows small worlds, each encircled by a complete ring, embroidered on his doublet.

1590—1600 (*continued*)

Ladies' stomachers or doublets were often cut from the same pattern as men's, and even at this early date we find the now time-worn assertion that women were aping men, and trying to appear masculine to the detriment of their natural charms. Though how a richly embroidered doublet with a lace-edged ruffle, worn over exaggeratedly full skirts, could be termed masculine it is difficult to comprehend.

Men's hair was worn frequently shoulder-length, and about 1595 a fashion for "ear-locks"—later termed love-locks—became very popular with young men. The hair in this case was allowed to grow in front so that it hung down in two locks, one either side of the face, and rested in a curl on each shoulder; the back, however, was kept short.

Practically any shape or size of hat might be fashionable during the 'nineties. High-crowned and small-brimmed, or low-crowned and large-brimmed, were each equally smart if worn with a cable hat-band. Some crowns were so high that they rose twelve or fifteen inches above the head. All colours and practically any material might be used in the making up of these hats.

1590—1600 (*continued*)

Trunk-hose with canions assumed two definite formations. One, the unbroken roll round the hips, as seen on several earlier pages, and the other somewhat square in effect, slightly resembling a miniature farthingale; three of these will be seen on the previous page. *Panes* either developed into a formal series of embroidered bands, with nothing of the padding or lining visible, or else became sufficiently small and narrow for the drawings-out to be evenly arranged to cover them. The latter arrangement gave the appearance of an equally-gathered piece of material, as is shown in the last coloured plate.

The skirt of the doublet at this time was cut up to form overlapping tabs similar in appearance to the "tassets" worn on armour. One other form of breeches that became a "rage" during the last decade of the century were the "open-breeches." These were perfectly straight, ungathered trousers, that reached a few inches below the knees, similar in cut to a rather elongated pair of modern shorts, or an abbreviated pair of trousers. Usually these were embroidered, and a tendency to decorate the hem with coloured ribbon or bone-lace ultimately developed into the lace-edged, flapping nether-garments of the Cavalier of the Stuart period.

1590—1600 (*continued*)

So we draw to the close of the most interesting century in our history, a century shaken by the discovery of a New World, yielding untold wealth for any man to exploit. The people, in their crazed enthusiasm over the New World, burst into wild orgies of expenditure. Illimitable adventure awaited them across the seas. Why should they be afraid of adventure in their own country? If a fortune were gambled away in one single night, what matter? Could not they sail forth, as others had done, to an unknown El Dorado, and come back in galleons laden with all manner of precious stones and great bars of gold and silver? No sober-minded stay-at-homes were they. And the spirit of adventure, bravery, and extravagance must needs be given expression—hence the dazzling array of costumes, the exotic materials, and the priceless decorations set forth in these pages.

English Costume of the Seventeenth Century

FOREWORD

ALTHOUGH the aim and scope of the books in this series are self-evident to most readers, it seems desirable to touch on two points in this connection. In the first place, they are not intended for, nor would they interest, those who have made a life-study of historic costume and who are primarily concerned with the intricacies of the subject. My purpose is to provide a useful guide and not a serious text-book, to give elementary descriptions of costume for those who have neither time nor inclination to pore over countless prints, paintings, and actual examples, yet who wish to obtain a comprehensive idea of the dress of the period. The condensation of any aspect of a whole century into less than one hundred pages necessitates so high a degree of selection that many of its omissions and inclusions equally are open to debate. Nevertheless, to those with slight knowledge of the subject, wishing to select costumes from a certain decade in history, a book of this size is infinitely more useful than a tome fifty times its weight and extent, which would certainly give more detail but probably fewer actual examples of the complete costume desired.

Secondly, it is clear that detail cannot be dealt with beyond a certain measure of accuracy in full-length drawings of three or four inches high when the figure from which the costume is taken is usually life-size and sometimes larger. A minute study of such details as collars, belts, shoes, gloves, and dozens of other equally interesting items can be made satisfactorily only in the excellent collections of the articles themselves, such as are found, for example, in several of the museums in and around London.

The Stuart period is perhaps the most romantic in English

history, a period in which men duelled and danced, fought hard and loved hard, with equal grace and accomplishment, in satins and lace. There was brutality enough and bitter feeling in the seventeenth century, war and suffering in abundance; yet contemporary portraiture has preserved a remarkable appearance of unruffled exquisiteness. These ghosts in wigs and ribbons, satins and silks, seem to live on more vividly than the historic facts with which they are surrounded—the Civil Wars of Cavalier and Roundhead, the Great Plague, the Fire of London, Monmouth's Rebellion, and the infamies of Judge Jeffreys. Memorable as these events were, those who took part in them, unrivalled in history in their apparently haughty indifference to plagues, fires, wars, and massacres, have left a more enduring impression, an impression of gay bravado reflected in and emphasized by their extravagance in clothes.

I. B.

1660

1600—1610

SO little change is remarkable during the first ten years of the seventeenth century, that it will be unnecessary to dwell upon each portion of the fashionable garments in detail. The century opens with the flamboyant and ungainly clothing of Elizabeth's Court. Stiff, bombasted, and doll-like, these figures in ruffles, farthingales, exaggerated breeches, and quilted garments leave a lasting picture on one's mind.

Anne of Denmark, the new Queen, has long been famed for her complete lack of taste in clothes, and in her hands rested the reformation, or otherwise, of the existing fashions. Unfortunately, her fancy led her to encourage and exaggerate the already hideous and deforming costumes then prevalent at Court. History informs us that on the death of Elizabeth, her ladies proceeded to Berwick, to greet James I's queen, laden with the jewels and gowns of their late-lamented queen. If we are to believe the reputed size of the virgin Queen's wardrobe, it is not inconceivable that Anne should have converted a few hundred, at least, of these costly and regal gowns to her own use. If this were the case, it might possibly explain the seeming lack of progress in fashion during the ensuing fifteen years!

The farthingale—ugliest of all modes—continued in fashion and increased in size, in spite of the King's bad-tempered endeavour to exterminate it, until the death of Anne in 1619. It appears that at a grand masque at Court, several of the ladies became wedged in the passage, and so completely blocked the entrance, that half or more of the guests never managed to get into the hall or attend the masque. After this tiresome experience, James issued a proclamation forbidding the farthingale to be worn at Court (" This impertinent garment takes up all the room at Court ") either by ladies or gentlemen—for the gallants not to be outdone by the fairer sex padded their breeches to a corresponding extent. No notice, however, was taken of this order, for the simple reason that the Queen flatly refused to abandon her favourite form of dress.

1600—1610 (*continued*)

Such fabulous sums were expended abroad on materials—silks, satins, velvets, etc., that one or two spirited endeavours were made to promote interest in the manufacture of materials at home. Mulberry farms were started in several parts of the country and silk-worms imported. Silk-growing survived for nearly a hundred years, and was only abandoned when the futility of protecting the mulberry trees in the chilly winter months was realized.

In the year 1599, William Lee, Master of Arts, at St. John's College, Cambridge, devised an " engine " or steel loom for knitting or weaving silk stockings, waistcoats, etc. From that date there were few ladies or gentlemen who denied themselves the luxury, comfort, and extravagance of silk stockings, even at £2 to £5 per pair.

The large sums paid for clothes seem out of all proportion to the salaries and incomes of the time. A plush cloak might cost £50; plush being sold at the ghastly price of £3. 10s. per yard (and exceedingly narrow it was, too); and of course, no garment was considered fit for a gentleman unless embroidered or guarded with lace or velvet. The importance of appearance may be seen in Ben Jonson's *Magnetic Lady*: " . . . He has stained my new white satin doublet and bespattered my spic and span silk stockings on the day they were drawn on, and here's a spot in my hose too "—this after a vulgar brawl.

Trimmings played just as important a part as they had during the sixteenth century; lace, ribbons, embroidery, artificial flowers, enamel, and jewels of all kinds, even coloured and gilded leather-work, were still placed indiscriminately on every garment—male or female. The Queen had a murrey-coloured satin gown ornamented with gilded cut leather sent her as a gift from the Queen of Spain. Breast-plates and collars of enamel and silver, or other fine metals, swords with embroidered and jewelled scabbards and sheaths, were frequently worn by men as part of their civil dress. Embroidered gloves, handsomely trimmed with fringe and tassels, were as necessary to the would-be élite as the embroidered and rosetted shoes.

1600—1610 (*continued*)

Long, loose gowns reaching to the ground, and trimmed with "shagg"—a long fur-like plush—or real fur, or even velvet, were worn by elderly gentlemen, or within the comparative privacy of one's own family circle. These gowns had the loose split sleeve, hanging from the shoulder, which formed the chief place of ornamentation. The breeches with canions, worn by the gentleman on the top right hand of the page facing, are composed entirely of heavy braid about an inch and a half to two inches wide—interlaced and sewn so as to leave a space through which a contrasting lining may be seen. With this form of nether-garment the stockings are tied just below the knees, and often hanging over the garter like the tops of boots. Over-stockings, with leather soles and embroidered tops; separate stocking-tops and boot-hose, were all worn at this period, and boots with coloured linings made of soft fancy leather were sometimes worn. It was not until the 'twenties, however, that the fashion was carried to an extreme. The large skirt-like breeches tended to elongate, giving them a squarish line at the knee, instead of the barrel shape of the earlier type; to bring the latter more up to date, tassels and ribbons were frequently attached at the knee.

A kind of slipper, similar to a mule, with a heel about an inch or more in height, was worn to a considerable extent within doors. Doublets and bodices of embroidered linen were worn by both sexes, and often caps or bonnets of similar design, and edged with lace, were made to match. There is an example of a lady wearing one of the caps at the bottom of the opposite page; and on the following page may be seen a gentleman in his indoor cap.

1600—1610 (*continued*)

Many and varied were the types of collar worn during this period—from the large Elizabethan ruffle to the flat lace collar worn by the little girl at the bottom of the second page of illustrations to this decade. A sufficiently comprehensive selection may be seen on these four pages.

In the year 1604 " James I by letter patents did incorporate the felt-makers of London, by the name of Hatter & Warders or Mistery of Feltmakers of London granting them divers privileges and liberties." Another endeavour to support home industries and thereby cut out the importation of Spanish and French beavers and felts! Men's hats were overwhelmingly large and covered in feathers and jewels—and correspondingly expensive! In Ben Jonson's *The Devil is an Ass*, the prize for a wager takes the form of " A new Four pound beaver hat, set with enamel studs." Any coloured hat was fashionable, although greys and blacks seemed most popular.

The hair-dressing or head-tiring of the ladies shows little or no difference from that of ten or even twenty-five years earlier. Quantities of jewellery was still worn in the hair, and saffron hair-dye remained a favourite tint. The black velvet hat with plumes of feathers still perched at an absurd angle on the back of the head, and any odd jewel or trinket that had not found a resting-place in my lady's periwig might be placed with impunity upon her hat!

1610—1620

ON the opposite page may be seen two excellent examples of the costumes of this period—the lady's taken from one of Anne's numerous portraits, and the other from a portrait of Henry, Prince of Wales. The extraordinary stiffness and impracticability of these clothes may be easily seen from these figures. It will be noticed that the bombasted breeches of the boy are split at the knee showing the lining—a fashion that became extremely prevalent during the 'twenties and 'thirties. The lined boots and boot-hose are also exceedingly advanced—as more of them are to be seen at a later date. The blue collar is an interesting point worthy of note, as, previously, collars had mostly been made of lawn, holland, or some white or natural-coloured material. The passion for decorating garments with gold braid or metal ribbon may be observed. Plain, indeed, was the doublet of this period if it were not ornamented with several yards of lace, embroidery, leather, bead-work, or braid. This suit was, in all probability, made of plush, of somewhat similar texture to the panne velvet of to-day.

This farthingale, similar to those worn by Elizabeth, was probably made according to the fashionable lady's requirements. " High at the back and low in the front, the sides wide, that I may rest my arms upon it." The collar was wired to keep it at the necessary angle to make a charming background to a well-painted picture !

Many hours' patient work were expended on my lady's toilet, many layers of clothes had to be fitted and fixed, and cosmetics had not yet arrived at any degree of perfection. The Spanish " papers " for rouge and powder did not arrive in England until many years later. A bag of chalk served the purpose of our modern powder-box !

1610—1620 (*continued*)

The last figure on this page has been specially inserted to show the arrangement of the skirt. To obtain the required outline, giant sausage-shaped horse-shoes of hair or rags were tied over the petticoat below the waist—the gown then being allowed to fall over this unwholesome piece of absurdity. This would account for the gown always being split up the front when the farthingale was worn, to facilitate the tying and arranging of the padding necessary to obtain the fashionable silhouette.

Ladies' hunting-suits or riding-habits of the day were not designed with the idea of giving any comfort to their wearers ; it was not even unusual to ride in a farthingale. If we are to take the portraits of the queen as typical of a fashionable lady's habit, we may perceive her dressed in a low revealing doublet, with stiff wired collar encircling the back of her head and neck, and making any neck movement difficult if not impossible. Full-padded sleeves split in the demands of fashion to expose the smock ; her skirts, if not actually concealing the farthingale—full-padded and trailing. An absurd hat of grey beaver, with a ridiculously high crown ornamented with feathers and enamel studs, perched unsafely on the front of her piled up hair.

The costume of the masked lady on the opposite page is also taken from a contemporary print of a group of ladies riding—although here the farthingale is small. It is difficult to imagine that a riding-suit of this sort could ever have been coped with, or worn with any degree of comfort. It will be noticed here that the lady is wearing a band under the chin—a device which appears to have accompanied the mask in various forms throughout the century. This particular mask was known as a Loo or half-mask.

Cuffs increased considerably during the decade, sometimes even being made in layers of three or four, and reaching above the elbow.

1610—1620 (*continued*)

An interesting variation of the immense breeches of the period may be observed at the top of the opposite page; these were cut on the lines of the open-breeches introduced some ten or fifteen years earlier, the gathering round the waist and the tightening of the hem giving a curious barrel effect. The doublet, too, is interesting in this example, as it shows a definite tendency to pad at the chest instead of having, as previously, all the padding near the belt. This latter fashion having survived in a much moderated form ever since the introduction of the Peas-cod doublet of the previous century.

After the death of Anne of Denmark, the ladies, having no leader to spur them on to further exaggerations and extravagances and no Court to dazzle with their magnificence, assumed a more subdued version of the previous fashions, and no longer vied with each other to wear the largest and most cumbersome petticoats, or the tallest head of hair most filled with jewels. And although one cannot, with any stretch of imagination, say that simplicity was the vogue, yet, after the extraordinarily bizarre and ostentatious fashions of the last quarter of a century, these ladies must have appeared amazingly subdued to one brought up in the wealthiest period of English History, and accustomed to the overdressed and over-bejewelled ladies and gentlemen at the Court of Good Queen Bess and the flamboyant Anne of Denmark.

From now onwards and until well into the eighteenth century the fairer sex held no light to the gallants in the matter of clothes. Every man had a thousand opportunities of adding a ribbon, a jewel, a fringe, a piece of lace, braid, rosette or curl; of showing an embroidered stocking, stocking-tips, costly boots, garters, and so on; whilst the woman must content herself with lace collars and cuffs, and perhaps a bunch of ribbons here or there.

1610—1620 (*continued*)

Beards and moustaches continued in favour until the 'eighties, and an amusing example of a beard, looking suspiciously artificial may be seen in the middle of the opposite page. The curly type of beard running round the chin to the jaw bones was most prevalent. This might be worn as in the picture of the man at the top of the page, or clipped to a point like that of the man at the bottom of the previous page. Men's hats had by now reached the height of their decoration—and price! Enamel studs and jewels of every kind found their place in the expensive hat-bands of the élite; and large metal or gold clasps, with coloured stones, were used to fix the feather decoration securely to the hat itself. So valuable were these hats that they were the first item to be removed by a highway thief or footpad. Men were lured within doors and their hats snatched before they had any idea who their assailant might be.

Gigantic pear-shaped pearls and stars, arrows, crescents, etc., were made in enamel and set with stones to wear in the hair. Pearls were so much worn at this time that even the edge of a collar might be closely set with these precious stones. The charming little lace-caps, already described, were not worn in England later than about 1618 or 1620. Caps were discarded for half a century or more in favour of a more elegant and informal type of hair-dressing. One notices that wherever the cap was worn in previous times the hair seemed to suffer in consequence. Few curls were allowed to escape from their hiding-place beneath layers of lace. Possibly the caps in history were invented for the busy woman who had no time for decorative hair-dressing, and just bundled up her hair beneath a cap, jammed on to hide any deficiencies.

1620—1630

THE first period of this decade was singularly lacking in advancement—or indeed any style at all. When the Queen died, James, devoid of feminine influence, had the Court cleared of women, and abandoned himself to drink and vice. The royal children had already been placed in the charge of various noblewomen about the country. The Court became a scene of carousing and debauchery, and fashions in England practically remained at a standstill. A few new modes filtered across the Channel, but until the vivacious and witty young Henrietta Maria arrived, bringing with her a Parisienne trousseau, the country had no one to lead them in fashions.

From the arrival on these shores in June 1625 of the daughter of France, a revolution in ladies' dress commenced. Gone were the farthingales, ruffles, and long stomachers. High short-waisted bodices with Medici collars, low revealing corsages, and soft silk petticoats reaching to the ground replaced the stiff brocaded, cheese-like short petticoats.

I have selected the garments on the opposite page—not because they are significant of 1620—but because they show a definite link between the new fashion and the old. The exact date of the woman's dress is probably about 1628, and the man's 1624. With the latter may be seen a shortening of the doublet together with an elongation of the "skirts" or "tassets"—the ruffle in its last form—breeches changing from the short "trunks" into knee-breeches with an ornamented hem.

The lady's dress still holds something of the stiffness of Elizabethan times—the long stomacher is there, but the new high waist-line is emphasized by a ribbon tied under the arm-pits. The petticoat is short—while the gown assumes the new length touching the ground. The hair is dressed in a definitely transitional stage; it is still crimped and drawn back from the forehead, but a tiny fringe is visible, and a few small curls are allowed to hang over the ears, which for several years had been displayed. Later it will be noticed the fringe developed into a row of neat curls, and the side-curls became more and more exaggerated until the 'nineties.

1620—1630 (*continued*)

Few of the drawings on these four pages represent clothes worn earlier than 1625, as the advancement between 1618 and 1625 was so slight. With Charles I comes a difference. Before the stereotyped dress associated with this unhappy king became prevalent, for a few years there was a slightly experimental stage. Doublets were many and varied in design; some in the French style with the square-cut skirts, so beautifully illustrated by Abraham Bosse, were introduced in about 1628. The leather jerkin, sleeveless and reaching half-way down the thigh, was worn by civilians as well as by the Militia of that time. These continued in favour until well into the 'sixties; sometimes they were devoid of decoration—sometimes fringed and ornamented at the hem and arm-holes.

Leg-wear by about 1627 or 1629 had taken the form of loose knee-breeches, tied or sewn down the side to within five or six inches of the knee, and from there to the garter gaping open to show the fine lining. An example of this may be seen on the top right-hand figure on the opposite page. Some of the breeches had fringe or lace at the knee, and often stockings with decorated stocking-tops were tied just below the knee, giving the same effect as an edge. These stocking-tops were worn over the ordinary stockings; the habit of wearing two or more pairs seems prevalent from about 1625 until the end of the century.

Boots and boot-hose increased in size and decoration—the bucket-topped boot becoming a necessary part of every would-be gallant's attire. Large flaps of a butterfly shape were worn over the instep of these monstrosities. Several contemporary satirists depict the fop straddling along in a ludicrous and ungainly walk impeded and finally tripped up by his enormous boots. Bows of ribbon and gigantic rosettes decorated the square, elongated toes of their shoes.

The rather attractive fashion of tucking up the petticoats was started towards the end of this decade—probably when the longer gowns were introduced and the ladies had some difficulty in negotiating the notoriously filthy streets without ruining their fine garments. At first the gowns were held up by hand, but later they were pinned or tied in a variety of fashions. The high-waisted, tabbed bodice diminished in length as it increased in width—the increased size of the sleeves and wide, pointed collars adding several inches to the shoulders of their wearers.

1620—1630 (*continued*)

Ladies' sleeves were often composed of three separate materials. First the sleeve of the "smock," or shift, of some fine holland or silk, and over this a multitude of ribbons reaching from shoulder to wrist tied below the elbow and revealing the lining as the ribbons fell from the arm. Over this ribbon was the short elbow-length sleeve belonging to the bodice or gown. This was cut to the epaulet on the shoulder in front and tied at the elbow, frequently reaching only across the back of the arm—as shown in the example at the top of the opposite page. The full sleeve was still worn a great deal, and there are a few examples before the 'thirties of a three-quarter length sleeve —as will be seen at the bottom of the opposite page. This style, however, did not become the rage until five or six years later.

On the previous page will be seen a girl in the peasant costume of the day. As this type of dress was worn for several years by the working-class, it will be unnecessary to frequently repeat it.

The period of lace had begun—lace cuffs, lace collars, lace at the wrist and knees, lace on gloves and stockings, lace even on hats, and every fine garment was "laced." Where previously a tiny edge of lace had been, a deep border took its place. Right through the century and well into the eighteenth the most beautiful and exquisite lace played an important part in the decoration of clothes.

1620—1630 (*continued*)

Veils became fashionable towards the end of the 'twenties. They were worn without a hat and consisted of a square piece of net laid over the head and reaching about as far as the mouth, the border often of lace. One of these is illustrated in the next group of heads (1630–1640). Hairdressing became more and more informal—the effect of nonchalance in the arrangement of the curls was belied by the neatness of the back-view. At first the hair was puffed at the sides, giving an effect of short hair from the front; later, the front curls were cut shorter, or added, in cases where nature had not been sufficiently generous for the demands of fashion. From this time onwards until the introduction of the pinner or commode in the late 'seventies, fashionable ladies wore no hats or head-dresses, with the exception of hoods, that were not equally suitable for men. The large beavers and felts, and even velvet caps, were exact replicas of their husband's or brother's.

Feathers decorated practically every hat. Long curling plumes of ostrich feathers stuck out from the hat-bands and drooped over the shoulders of the gallants, mingling with their locks, now worn long. The shoulder-length curls were now allowed to grow several inches over the collar. Some of the older men still adhered to the mode of short hair, but men of all ages wore the fashionable Van Dyck beard and moustaches, the brighter sparks curling their moustaches to ridiculous extremes, and clipping their beards to a sharp point.

The ruffle, having quite disappeared by 1627, was supplanted by the now famous Van Dyck collar. Made of the most exquisite lace, they reached from the throat to points over the shoulders. The stiffened pleated Medici collar remained in favour until the 'fifties.

1630—1640

THE cut of the doublet on the opposite page is typical of the 'thirties. Often the front was slashed in two or three places to show the shirt. The breeches were tied to the doublet at this time, with points threaded through the eyelet holes round the waist above the tabs or tassets. The epaulet was still worn on the shoulders of every doublet. Sleeves varied only slightly, all being formed of ribbons reaching from shoulder to wrist. Sometimes they were joined just below the elbow, and the forearm in this case was tightly fitting, but usually they hung loosely, showing large puffs of silk shirt. Cuffs were all made of lace or embroidered linen. The collar was edged with fine lace; in this instance it is supported round the face, although this type of collar was rarely seen after 1630, the popularity of the Van Dyck collar sweeping other modes before it.

Children of either sex wore these charming little caps until they were four or five years old, little girls wearing them until they were eight or ten years of age. The pinafore or apron, decorated with fine lace, was worn by little girls throughout the entire century.

The embroidered bodice of the lady is very similar in design to that of her spouse—the same type of sleeve being equally fashionable for either sex. The ladies' costumes at this period were very subdued in contrast to those worn ten or twenty years earlier. Plain materials were more to be seen than patterned, and a lace collar and cuffs were often the only form of adornment.

The Queen was not extravagant in clothes, the duties of a mother claiming all her attention. In one of her letters she writes to France asking for a new petticoat-bodice, as she has nothing but a velvet one which she had two years previously, and that is worn and too short and tight to be fashionable. This modest request stands out in history after the ridiculous quantities of garments the two previous queens had indulged in. Of all the accusations hurled at this unhappy Queen, nothing could be said about her personal extravagance. The only other mention of wearing apparel in Henrietta Maria's letters seems to have been a request for one dozen pairs of sweet chamois gloves and one of doeskin.

1630—1640 (*continued*)

By 1630 all signs of padding and stuffing in the breeches had disappeared. They now hung loosely, fitting the leg to the knee, where they were usually tied with a lengthy and wide garter wound several times round the leg, and then tied in a large bow or arranged as a rosette. Boots continued in size and decorativeness and were rarely worn without the boot-hose, or stocking-tops, hanging over the turned-down top. The figure of the small boy at the top of the page is taken from a portrait of William of Orange, and it is interesting to note that as early as '39, the short coat was worn in the Netherlands, when it did not become prevalent in England until the 'forties. This example has the sleeves and slashing of the 'thirties, also the collar.

Ladies' hair was worn longer than previously, "heart-breakers," or long curls, being arranged to fall over the shoulders. Hair ornaments of pearls and ribbon were worn a great deal at either side of the "bun" at the back, and showing from the front. Little girls wore, what would to-day be called hair-ribbons, to tie their curls back from their forehead—as may be seen at the top of the opposite page.

The stomacher was nearly always cut in a U shape below the waist. The neck-line of the bodice no longer formed a V in front, a square being much more fashionable. This was usually very low cut, and often a tiny frill of lace protruded from the top of the bodice. Long strings of pearls were exceedingly fashionable, often being worn to emphasize the waist-line, and tied in a variety of fashions at the neck and waist.

Cuffs might fall softly from the three-quarter length sleeve or they might turn back, their "raggs" or points reaching to the elbow. Furs, stoles, or tippets were worn during the 'thirties; and the first umbrella appeared in England in this decade.

1630—1640 (*continued*)

So many are the brilliant drawings of Abraham Bosse, the son of a French tailor, and Wenceslaus Hollar during this period, that it is extremely difficult to make a selection of typical garments from the vast quantities available. The French and English styles differ a little, but as both must have been worn in England—Henrietta Maria never forgetting unfortunately that she was a Frenchwoman—both styles must be represented. The muff tied in the centre with ribbon, and the box-pleated petticoat are both amusing and unexpected. The mock-sleeves on the little child's gown are unusual at so advanced a period of the seventeenth century.

Capes, from the 'thirties onwards, were an indispensable part of every man's attire, and they were worn *under* the collar of the doublet. Hats became larger and with higher crowns as the 'forties approached. The French method of men's hairdressing consisted of a fuzzy bush of untidy curls around the face and head with several long curls hanging down the back; whilst in England the more favourite method of dressing the hair was in a long curly "bob," resting on the collar in a layer of well-ordered ringlets. Moustaches and beards continued in favour, and varied but slightly from the style of ten years earlier.

The little maid-servant at the bottom of the page has her hair tucked away in a cap—one of the few examples of a cap of any sort worn during this period. She is fixing the extra collar on her mistress's dress. These collars were worn over the square-shaped ones, and in many contemporary portraits it is possible to see right through the outer collar of fine material to the neckline of the dress itself, which was always square in front.

Furs, gloves, masks, hoods, and veils were all important etceteras of the ladies' possessions. An interesting item which was worn from about 1630 to the end of the century was the little shoulder-cape, worn whilst the hair was being arranged and with practically any form of deshabille.

1630—1640 (*continued*)

The first example here is the back view of the French fashion in men's hairdressing—a bow of ribbon is here attached to the longest lock. This craze for odd bows of ribbon in the hair—ornamental perhaps, but entirely useless—remained fashionable for about thirty years, in fact until the periwig took the place of natural hair.

Black net veils were worn to protect the ladies' complexions from the harmful rays of the sun. Freckles and sunburn were considered harmful and disfiguring. To our minds this careful covering of the face, but exposure of the neck and head to the full blaze of the summer sunshine seems particularly stupid; no doubt, however, the lily-skinned beauties of the 1630's would regard our sun-tanned faces as distinctly unladylike and probably indecent.

During the winter months, still greater care was taken to prevent the skin from being roughened or exposed to the chilly winds. A hood completely encircling the face was worn, a mask covered the forehead and nose, and a chin-band was snugly arranged to conceal the jaw, so that the entire face was hidden except the mouth. Furs were worn extensively so that the ladies could snuggle under them, as we do to-day, in the teeth of an East Wind. It is questionable whether their complexions really benefited by all this tender care, but if their skins were soft and peach-like, it is, alas! impossible for us now to discover, or we might possibly be persuaded to follow in their footsteps.

The large flat-brimmed beaver or felt hat was first seen in about 1638. This style afterwards developed into the high-crowned hats of the 'forties, and the large Puritan hats worn by the Parliamentary party must have been designed from one similar to the example on the opposite page.

1640—1650

THE 'forties were turbulent and restless years; the Civil Wars breaking up the country into two distinct parties, each with their own dress, and each going to opposite extremes with their exaggerations.

The gown and suit on the opposite page show the somewhat moderated gloom of civil attire, though the man is definitely of Cavalier tendencies, judging by the bows of ribbon on his love-locks. These clothes also show the short-lived popularity of the sober dress associated with this period.

Mrs. Hutchinson, in the *Memoirs* of her husband, says: "When Puritanism grew into a faction the zealots distinguished themselves, both men and women, by several affections of habit, looks, and words, which had it been a real declension of vanity and embracing of sobriety in all those things had been most commendable in them; but their quick forsaking of those things when they were where they would be showed that they either never took them up for conscience' sake or were corrupted by their prosperity to take up those vain things they durst not practice under persecution. Among other affected habits, few of the Puritans, whatsoever degree they were of, wore their hair long enough to cover their ears, and the ministers and many others cut it close round their heads, with so many little peaks as was ridiculous to behold—from this custom of wearing hair the name of roundhead became the scornful term given to the whole Parliament party." Colonel Hutchinson wore his hair long and curled—and, indeed, had a very fine head of hair, fanatical Puritan though he was. We may also suppose that he did not affect the ordinary Puritan garb, as his wife speaks of a handsome red velvet doublet of his.

1640—1650 (*continued*)

The Cavaliers took good care that they should not be mistaken for the opposing party, and exaggerated every fashion to the point of ridicule. The short coat, barely reaching to the waist, displayed quantities of fine shirt—and ribbons were attached to the hems of every garment. Breeches—which had assumed the proportions of a skirt by the 'fifties, were, for the most part, knee-length, and hung loose, the better to show off layers of ribbon or lace. The sides often had bows or rosettes attached—this form of ornamentation eventually resolving itself into a panel of lace or ribbon, or both, from waist to hem. The tighter form of knee-breeches was still worn, and embroidered stockings, tied up or pinned above the knee on to the breeches, were often seen, as in the figures on the top right hand of the opposite page.

Both these figures are wearing clothes more suitable to the Parliamentarians than the Royalists. Capes were extensively worn during this period, and it was also during the 'forties that the ladies' waist-line once more dropped to normal; the exaggerated sleeves became less inflated and the neck-line lower. A curious item about the Puritan collar is worthy of note: the collar seems to have been an entirely separate affair, pinned at the throat and dropping over the shoulders, the Λ-shaped space in front revealing a low-necked bodice with an expanse of uncovered chest. One of these collars is worn by Elizabeth Cromwell in a contemporary miniature, and, although she wears the traditional Puritan bonnet, her hair beneath is revealed in careful ringlets.

Long aprons of finest lawn with a tiny lace edge became a part of fashionable attire during this period; previously they had been worn only by children and domestics. A loose shoulder-cape was often worn by ladies to give additional warmth, and muffs and furs played an important part in every winter wardrobe.

1640—1650 (*continued*)

At the bottom of the opposite page will be seen a messenger boy or page in his trunk-hose. This form of nether garment was worn throughout the century by page-boys and as a Court-dress on a great many occasions.

The subdued tone and comparative simplicity of the ladies' attire at this time was probably due to the dangers a well-dressed woman was exposed to should any Parliamentarian set foot in her house. Any form of ostentation, for a few years at least, was viewed with definite disfavour.

The Cavalier light-heartedly stepped into the fray, taking an absurd delight in showing his bravery and royalty, though trammelled with feathers, lace, and love-locks. His absurd boots probably impeded him, but rather than discard one item of finery he preferred to flaunt his allegiance to the sovereign as long as the King drew breath.

In contrast a contemporary writer describes the Parliamentary party: "In high-crowned hats, collar bands, great loose coats, with long swords under them, and calves' leather boots."

The absurd fashions eventually triumphed over the more sedate fashions favoured by the Parliamentarians, and, as Mrs. Hutchinson mentions in her *Memoirs*, if any one had seen the "Roundheads" even a couple of years after their first heated demonstration of Purity—it would have been impossible to see the reason for their name.

1640—1650 (*continued*)

Ladies of Royalist inclination wore their hair in a long thick mass of curls, covering their shoulders and adorned with numerous bows of ribbon. As will be seen in the figure on the previous page, the back hair was still neatly arranged. The lady with the curls on the opposite page happens to be taken from a contemporary miniature of Cromwell's daughter, Mrs. Ireton, so that despite her Puritan tendencies her vanity was not sufficiently subdued for her to abandon and forsake her curls, in favour of the Puritan cap; neither do her scantily-draped shoulders indicate the modesty required of Ireton's wife. Altogether, after studying the period, these Parliamentarians seem to have been a set of fanatical humbugs—with the exception, of course, of the Puritan Fathers, who were so disgusted with the vanities and immorality in England. They set themselves a rigid and austere code of life, and abandoned the country so saturated with vice, for a new World where they could practise what they believed, untrammelled by the persecution and ridicule to which sobriety and modesty had previously exposed them.

In the year 1649 Cromwell passed an Act "For the relief of felt-makers and hat-band-makers against aliens and strangers." In spite of James I's efforts, apparently, to promote the hat industry in England, foreign competition was again getting the upper hand. It is curious that Cromwell should interest himself in anything so trivial during the year of the execution of the unhappy Charles.

It is recorded in Henrietta Maria's *Memoirs* that it was she herself who originally gave the name of "Roundhead" to the Cromwellian party. Seeing for the first time this curious fashion in a Parliamentary demonstration, and being struck by one of their number, she remarked: "La! What a handsome roundhead!"

1650—1660

ENGLAND during the Commonwealth gives one the impression of sobriety and modesty, yet curiously enough, if we are to believe the writers—or the artists—of that day, though the latter are more conspicuous by their absence than at any other period in history, England continued to light-heartedly proceed in her extravagances and fopperies. Even without the evil example of the extravagant and reckless Court, and in spite of the crushing and bigoted influence of the Protector, the majority of the men still wore their hair long and curled, and had bows of ribbon tied to their love-locks. Ladies still wore patches on their faces to attract attention to their dimples, or other attractive features, and, what is even more extraordinary and unexpected, we learn from an entry in *Evelyn's Diary* in the year 1654: ". . . I now observed how the women began to paint themselves, formerly a most ignominous thing and only used by prostitutes."

In the entry above this surprising piece of news we learn that he did "Visit the Mulberry Gardens, now the only place of refreshment about towne for persons of the best quality to be exceedingly cheated at; Cromwell and his partisans having shut up and seized on Spring Gardens, which till now had been the usual rendezvous of ladies and gallants at this season." This hardly strengthens or confirms the idea of the domesticated and reformed ladies and gentlemen, virtuously renouncing the "pomps and vanities of this world," especially as John Evelyn was an excellent and worthy gentleman of a religious turn of mind.

On the opposite page will be seen the, to us laughable, habit of the dashing gallant. His absurd jacket still retains something of the tasseted skirts in the form of two-inch flaps—these flaps disappeared entirely during the 'fifties. The turned-up hat was decorated equally on both sides: a frill of lace laid round the edge of the brim and a large bunch of coloured ribbons balancing the feathers on the other side.

1650—1660 (*continued*)

Several entries from the *Diary* of Samuel Pepys in the year 1659 give us an idea of the importance attached to clothes at this period—especially those worn by this amusing humbug himself. Remembering that Pepys was the son of a tailor, and therefore as appropriately attired as the figures illustrated by Abraham Bosse, also the son of a tailor, twenty or thirty years previously, one must consider him as a definite authority on the subject.

On January 1, 1659, he writes: "This morning I rose, put on my suit with great skirts, having not lately worn any other clothes but them." (This is probably similar to the last suit on the opposite page.) However, the same suit was discarded the following month in favour of "My white suit with silver lace coat," and about the same time he wears a "Jackanapes coat with silver buttons"; none of which sound at all Puritanical. He presents his wife with £5, to buy herself a petticoat (after spending three or four times as much on himself), and receives an unpleasant shock when she returns to him and, apparently innocently, tells him that his father has persuaded her to buy a fine cloth at twenty-six shillings a yard, and please may she have some more money as it must have some fine lace upon it! On the following Sunday he expresses his regret that the petticoat "makes no great show," being "light coloured and lace all over silver." But he takes care that she treats this expensive garment with due care, and severely reprimands her when she leaves it untidily in the bedroom. This historian tells us that shoes were exceedingly uncomfortable when new, and he frequently records the agony of wearing a new pair of shoes. One entry describes their walk to church with his wife wearing new footwear: "My wife exceedingly troubled by a pair of new pattens and I vexed to go so slow."

1650—1660 (*continued*)

Riding-habits seem to have been exactly similar to men's suits. A lady's riding-habit described by Pepys several years later, was probably designed in a similar manner to the example opposite. He writes: "Walking in the galleries I find the Ladies of Honour dressed in their riding garbs, with coats and doublets with deep skirts, just for all the world like mine, and buttoned their doublets up the breast, with perriwig and with hats: so that, only for a long petticoat dragging under their men's coats, nobody could take them for women in any point whatever; which was an odd sight, and a sight did not please me." The effeminacy of his own clothing obviously did not strike him. Probably these suits were similar to the one on page 53.

Men's heads, before the fashion for periwigs became general, were decorated and curled to ridiculous extremes. Each curl that fell over the gallant's shoulder must be adorned with a bow of ribbon—sometimes even the back curls were divided and tied. The crowns of hats were often eight or nine inches in height, and the brims received divers attentions in the complicated arrangements of ribbons, lace, feathers, and plumes.

1650—1660 (*continued*)

In contrast the ladies' heads must have seemed small; curls were not worn to any great excess, unless the wearer was blessed with natural curls, the hair being dressed with merely a slight wave and rarely reaching lower than the chin. Fine jewels and pearls still adorned the head, but it was not until after the Restoration that the hair was extravagantly dressed. The back-view of the hood on the opposite page shows how it was gathered to allow the kiss-curls at the nape of the neck to be clearly seen.

It is probable that as widows were so much in evidence during this decade that the heavy weeds worn previously became an unwarrantable expense and an indication of their political inclinations. At all events, the charming little peaked black cap with the white lining became a fashionable and exceedingly attractive form of mourning. The heavy veiling was probably rejected by the Royalists as being too sombre to express their extravagant views, and too similar to the dreary uniform adopted by the Puritan fanatics.

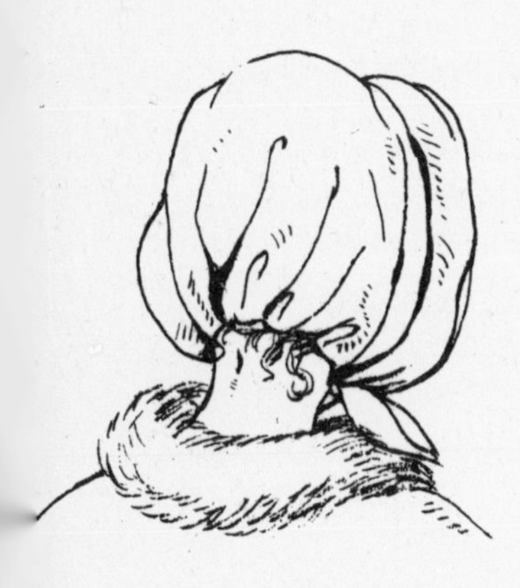

1660—1670

WITH the arrival of Charles II into England, and the reinstallation of a Court—fresh outbursts of wild gaiety and rejoicings led the country into a whirl of thoughtless extravagance and immorality.

John Evelyn writes of the King's coronation in 1661: "Clad in the fantastig habits of the time the magnificent traine or horseback, as much as embroidery, velvet, cloth of gold and silver, and jewels, could make them and their pransing horses, proceeded through the streets strewed with flowers, houses hung with rich tapestry, windoes and balconies full of ladies."

The same spirit of intoxication seems to have continued for several years, and with it the squandering of vast sums upon clothes and articles of adornment.

Curiously enough the men far surpassed the women in their overdressing—some of the ladies looking positively sombre in contrast to the feathered, laced, and beribboned gallants. Rather charming were the little black velvet coats edged with white fur of Dutch origin, as worn by the lady in the frontispiece page. Their simplicity strikes a quaint note in contrast to the ladies' flowered and laced garments. Lace played such an important part in the clothes of the day that no lady wished to be without at least one gown "laced all over."

Pepys has great difficulty with his wife in this particular. After forbidding her to go to the extravagance of buying one of these gowns—her new one arrives covered in lace, and her old one also appears with narrow lace "all over"—she seemingly surprised at this error! Pepys also notes on August 29, 1660: "This is the first day that ever I saw my wife with black patches since we were married." Patches had, however, been introduced towards the end of Charles I's reign.

Both long coats and "jackinapes," or short waist-length coats, were worn at this period. Some of the latter type of suit were carried to ridiculous absurdity—as in the example at the bottom of the opposite page. Ribbons of several different shades were worn on the same garment, or sometimes embroidered ribbons or multi-coloured ribbons.

The collars of the suits at this time continued to be high and stiffened—the cravat being worn over the coat and entirely separate.

1660—1670 (*continued*)

In the year 1665 Evelyn (according to himself) suggests a new mode of attire after the "Eastern Fashion," which the King light-heartedly adopts for a short time. Unfortunately no examples of this type of dress remain, although both Pepys and Rugge mention it. Evelyn's records on October 18 of this year: "To Court. It being the 1st time his Majesty put himself solemnly into the Eastern Fashion of vest, changeing doublet, stiff collar, bands, and cloake, into a comely vest, after the Persian mode, with girdle or straps, and shoe-strings and garters into bouckles of which some were set with precious stones, resolving never to alter it, and to leave the French mode, which had hitherto obtained to our greate expense and reproch. Upon which divers courtiers and gentlemen gave his Majesty gold by way of wager that he would not persist in resolution." And by the 30th of that month he had himself adopted these clothes: "To London to our office, and I had on the vest and surcoat or tunic as 'twas call'd, after his Majesty had brought the whole court to it. It was a comely and manly habit, too good to hold, it being impossible for us in good earnest to leave the Monsieurs vanities long." Pepys describes the "Eastern Fashion": "Being a long cassocke close to the body, of black cloth, and pinked with white silk under it, and a coat over it and legs ruffled with black riband like a pigeon leg."

And Rugge: "Viz. a close coat of cloth pinkt with a white taffety under . . . This in length reached the calf of the leg, and upon that a surcoat cutt at the breast, which hung loose and shorter than the vest 6 inches. The breaches of the Spanish cut, and buskins some of cloth some of leather, but of the same colour as the vest or garment."

Possibly this attire was similar to the long coats worn by young boys. Boys frequently remained long-coated until they reached the age of twelve or thirteen. I have not here illustrated this fashion; it is sufficient to say that it closely resembles the coats still worn by the Blue Coat boys to-day.

The fashion in England of wearing the skirts tucked up, tied up, and pinned up, continued in favour throughout the century, and was an excellent excuse for ladies to wear two beautiful petticoats instead of one.

The waist-line continued to move downward. Jewellery—especially pearls, were necessary accessories to any well-dressed woman. Pepys buys his wife a necklace of pearls—three rows for £80, and another at an earlier date for £4, 10s., so that apparently any price might be paid for these baubles.

1660—1670 (*continued*)

Periwigs became more and more prevalent, in the year 1663, Pepys has his hair cut—buys a periwig for £4, and has his own hair made into another for 25s. Ladies wore them only in riding-dress, and then over their own hair. Frequently, however, artificial curls were worn attached to the sides of the head. Hats were still large and decorated with feathers, although as the 'seventies approach the tall hat becomes less fashionable, and the large-brimmed hat with a low crown increases in favour. This hat was the forerunner of the tricorn worn throughout the eighteenth century. By about 1670 some of the hats took on a definitely three-cornered aspect.

Feminine head-dressing was somewhat severe at this period, the hair being drawn back from the face and arranged in an oval "bun" at the back—the "bun" being tied each side with ribbons, or decorated with gems or artificial flowers. Curls were worn at the side of the face resting on the shoulders, and a short-curled fringe or sometimes a row of tiny curls adorned the forehead—these were termed "Cruches."

Hats were rarely worn by the fairer sex—the hood disarranging the hair less, and infinitely more camouflaging should the owner wish to go abroad masked to an illicit rendezvous. With cloak, hood, mask, and fan, little or no chance of recognition was possible.

It will be noticed from the accompanying illustrations that ladies' neckwear was either *décolleté* in the extreme or the exact reverse—one's collar was either to one's throat or else did not begin till after the shoulders were exposed; in either case lace or fine net must be the only material used.

Pepys mentions his "Best black cloth suit trimmed with scarlet ribbon, very neat, and my cloake lined with velvet—a new beaver, which altogether is very noble with my black silk knit canions"—canions in this case meaning the overstockings worn loose and dropping down like a boot, and similar to the examples on the previous page. In 1668 he puts on "A New Stuff suit with a shoulder belt according to the new fashion and the bands of my vest tunique laced with silk lace of the same colour." These shoulder bands may also be observed in the drawings.

Black was an exceedingly fashionable colour; Pepys mentions several black suits of his, and a black silk dress of his wife's "laced all over with black lace point."

1670—1680

THE period of the short coat had definitely come to an end by about the year 1668. The long-skirted type of coat once installed, remained in favour for over a century. These coats were first worn with a belt or sash tied round the waist, and a long waistcoat of varying length reaching from shoulder to the middle of the thigh, or to the bottom of the coat was specially fashionable. Breeches were often made of black velvet, contrasting with a coloured coat, and these continued to be ornamented with ribbons, lace, and fringe for several years after the installation of the skirted coat. Ornamental sword belts, or shoulder belts as they were often termed, were worn a great deal as part of the necessary civil dress. The sleeve of the coat rarely reached below the elbow, and was turned back in an elaborate cuff—cut in a variety of complicated designs. Often the waistcoat had long sleeves, and these were sometimes turned back over the cuff of the coat-sleeve. Occasionally they were worn tight nearly to the wrist, from whence the luxurious lace-frills of the shirt bunched out in a cascade of lace and silk. Ribbons were still worn at shoulder, elbow, and knee, and beautiful embroideries adorned the split skirt at the back of the coat, down the facings and the pockets. The cravat was usually tied with a small bow of ribbon—this fashion later developed into the stiff formal arrangement of scarlet ribbons.

The periwig took on vast proportions during the 'seventies, and increased in size until about 1710—when it was supplanted by the white wig. Boots were not often worn except for riding—the fashionable form of footwear being that with a high tongue or flap reaching from four to six inches above the instep.

The gentleman on the opposite page has his " flaps " cut in an ornamental fashion, and falling down over the buckle; these were usually lined with silk or a contrasting shade of leather. Heels were high and sometimes red. An excellent example of the type of breeches worn on the opposite page may be seen at the Victoria and Albert Museum.

1670—1680 (*continued*)

Ladies' fashions definitely changed during the 'seventies. Not only the hairdressing, but practically every item altered slightly. Trains were often worn at Court, and at other times the skirts were drawn back in a somewhat formal manner giving the effect of a bustle. The fashionable bodice was very tight and low-waisted, with a tiny sleeve either pinned up or turned back well above the elbow. High collars were not so prevalent as the low neckline dropping off the shoulders at the side and forming a V in front. Flowered taffety, moire, and flowered tabby were favourite materials—floral patterns being more in use from the 'seventies onwards than previously, and a patterned material was more usual than one decorated with lace and ribbons. All these silks were exquisitely embroidered by hand, and the designs were amazingly naturalistic in manner. So beautiful were these minute posies that it seems almost incredible to us in this age of hustle and bustle that any human being could find the time and have the inexhaustible patience to cover dozens of yards of silk with almost invisible stitches.

The smocks or under-garments at this period had immense bunched and gathered sleeves—infinitely fuller than those of the bodice and always decorated with a deep frill of lace or embroidery. Several hundred illustrations would be an inadequate reference to seventeenth-century ornamentation. Unfortunately there is no opportunity for even a few examples of small details of lace and embroidery ornamentation to be inserted in these pages, but should the reader be sufficiently interested, dozens of interesting examples of the exquisite needlework executed by our industrious ancestors will be found in the Victoria and Albert Museum.

1670—1680 (*continued*)

Gloves of an elbow length were again introduced about 1670 and worn on practically every occasion. The hood and mask still played an important part in every wardrobe, and the frilled beribboned " pinner " was first seen on these shores in the late 'seventies. Muffs, furs, sunshades, tippets —more often termed " Palatines "—painted fans, velvet shoes, long gloves, and embroidered stockings were all necessary etceteras.

The complexion received more attention than hitherto. Lily-white hands were acquired by the wearing of chicken-skin gloves at night. " Plumpers " were added to sunken cheeks, these were small balls of some flexible substance, jammed into the mouth, and poked up into the cheeks to give their wearers a youthful and chubby facial contour.

Many and varied were the styles in masculine head-gear, including the flat-brimmed, low-crowned beaver similar to that at the top of the opposite page. The high-crowned style with many feathers arranged at the back was the French mode, and not worn later than about 1672. Many varieties of the tricorn were also popular, and the fashion for turning the brim right back from the face and lining the edge with ostrich feathers was extremely prevalent.

1670—1680 (*continued*)

When Charles II's youngest sister arrived in England in the year 1670, she brought with her in her train the famous mistress of Louis XIV, Madame de Queraille. This beautiful woman wore her hair dressed in an entirely new mode —similar to that in the centre of the opposite page. The sides of the hair were curled and puffed and brushed out in a mass of small ringlets, whilst the centre parting and flatness on the top of the head remained in sharp contrast to the bunched sides; the back hair was worn long, and drawn over the shoulders in several ringlets. Many pictures of the famous Court beauties have their hair dressed after this fashion—including Nell Gwynne.

The little lace caps were very fashionable. They were always adorned with a bow of ribbon in the front, and the hair was curled and cut so as to form a massive fringe of curls over the forehead. The back hair was drawn back and tied in a gigantic "boss" or bundle, called a choux. This was a very charming fashion, but seems to have been more in favour in France than in England. Madame Fontange wore the first top-knot; which was named after her.

Lace veils were often worn over the head, and so were hoods. No method of hairdressing provided for ladies with straight hair, so the curling irons played a great part in the head-tiring of the time, and also the "Tour" or artificial bunch of curls on the forehead.

1680—1690

HERE is seen the amazing use of ribbon during the 'eighties; dozens of yards must have been required to tie the front of this lady's corsage, and hardly less to decorate her swain's wrists, shoulders, hat, throat, sword, and garters. The gown is made of flowered tabby and decorated with fine black net lace. The gathered frill at the feet was extremely fashionable, and so was the fringe at the hem, or a deep band of inserted lace or embroidery. Her companion is wearing a suit of black cloth, with a flowered tabby vest and gold lace at the hands. His "mouchoir" decorated with fine lace hangs gracefully from his otherwise entirely ornamental pockets—"handkerchief" was considered a vulgar word at this period! The ribbons on his coat are scarlet, also the dozens of buttons.

The daughter of Evelyn the diarist gives such a wonderful description of the fashionable lady in her *Voyage into Maryland; or, The Ladies' Dressing-Room Unlocked*, that any other description would seem futile. She satirically records the bare necessities a wife will demand of her poor deluded husband:

"... Of Poïnt d'Espagne a rich Cornet,
Two night-Rails, and a Scarf beset
With a great Lace, a Collaret.
One black gown of Rich Silk, which odd is
Without one Colour'd, Embroider'd Bodice.
Four Petticoats for Page to hold up,
Four short ones nearer to the Crup:
Three Manteaus nor can Madam leſs
Provision here for due undreſs.
Nor demy Sultane, Spagnolet,
Nor Fringe to sweep the Mall forget:
Of under Bodice—3 neat pair
Embroidered, and of Shoos as fair:
Short under Petticoats pure fine,
Some of Japan Stuff, some of Chine.
With knee hight Galoon bottomèd,
Another quilted White and Red;
With a broad Flanders Lace below:
Four pair of Bas de foy shot through
With silver, Diamond Buckles too,
For Garters, and as Rich for show.
Twice twelve day smocks of Holland fine,

1680—1690 (*continued*)

With cambric sleeves, rich Points joyn
(For she despises Collertine).
Twelve more for night, all Flanders lac'd,
Or else she'll think her self disgraced.
The same her Night-gown must adorn,
With two Point Waistcoats for the morn:
Of Pocket Mouchoirs hope to drain,
A dozen lac'd, a dozen plain.
Three night Gowns of rich Indian Stuff,
Four Cushion-Cloths are ſcarce enough
of Point, and Flanders, nor forget
Slippers embroidered on Velvet. . . ."

Here is a glossary of some of the terms used above, with a few of the other quaint but interesting terms in use at the time:

Rayonne — Upper hood, pinn'd in Circle like the Sun-Beams.
Raggs — Names used for all sorts of Point Lace, etc.
Spannish paper — A beautiful red colour, ladies in Spain use for rouge.
Sprunking — A narrow sleeved gown.
Sultane — A gowne trimmed with buttons or loops.
Surtout — Night Hood covering the entire dress.
Pennache — A bunch or tassel of small ribbon.
Echelles — Stomacher laced with ribbons.
Campaine — A narrow picked lace.

One must visualize the dainty gentlemen of this time drinking chocolate, taking snuff, and nonchalantly combing their periwigs in public:

". . . Fops and men of wigs and snuff,
Knights of the famous Oyster Barrel Muff."

1680—1690 (*continued*)

Muffs were worn by all fashionable gentlemen after about 1688–89. They were immense things, and attached to their wearers' waists by a wide belt and a large ring to which they were sewn. One of these may be seen on the page opposite.

The full-skirted coats were cut with a decided " waist," somewhat lower than the natural waist-line, and pleats or gores were inserted to give extra width to the skirts. The pockets which had originally served a useful purpose were now merely a place for added ornament and embroidery—frequently even these so-called pockets were non-existent, consisting of a band of some contrasting stuff or embroidery sewn on to the coat skirts, often only a few inches from the hem of the coat, and completely out of reach of the hands. Buttons were worn in large quantities on both vest and coat, and often the sleeves were decorated with them.

Breeches became tighter, and by about 1685 had ceased to be at all ornamental—in fact, they were no longer visible beneath the long-skirted coat. Stockings were worn drawn up over the knee and gartered just below; sometimes two garters were worn, one above the knee and one below. Buckles on shoes took the place of the earlier bow or tie, and heels were worn even higher than during the 'seventies.

Flirting gracefully over a painted fan, their ladies also supped the fashionable chocolate or their cups of coffee. Their faces were patched, powdered, and rouged, and their hair arranged in a multitude of curls—each and every one with a different name. And piled upon their heads a variety of lace and ribbon conglomeration known as the " commode"—this will be dealt with later. So complicated was this " commode " that it attracted the jeering attention of every satirist and poet of the period. In her *Mundus Muliebris*, Evelyn's daughter remarks after a complicated description of head-tiring:

> " Thus face that erst near head was plac'd,
> Imagine now about the waist!

A passion for spot patterns, stripes, and plaids prevailed in ladies' clothes during the 'eighties and 'nineties, and fringe was used as an adornment to any garment. The " Echelles " or stomacher laced with ribbon was more fashionable than the plain bodice. Skirts became fuller as the period advanced towards the 'nineties, trains frequently being worn.

1680—1690 (*continued*)

No lady was seen abroad without her head dressed up in the most extraordinary manner. Patching was carried to ridiculous extremes—the mouche was often worn not only on the face but on the neck and shoulders. These patches were cut in a variety of shapes—stars, moons, etc., being the simplest and most usual forms.

One of the delightful satires of the period includes a minute description of head-tiring; unfortunately so much of it requires translation that a complete dictionary of the period is necessary. However, a small portion of these head arrangements will be found on the following pages, with a minute glossary for those who are interested:

> " The Settee, Cupée place aright
> Frelange, Frontange, Favourite,
> Monte la haut, and Palifade,
> Sorti, Flandan (great helps to trade),
> Burgoigne, Jardiné, Cornett.
> Frilal next upper Pinner fet . . ."

Pinner — A fan-shaped, pleated frill standing up in the front of the bonnet.
Settee — The double pinner.
Cupée — A special kind of pinner.
Frelange — The bonnet and pinner together.
Frontage — Top knot.
Favourite — Locks on temple.
Monte la haut — The wire to raise the head-dress.
Palifade — A wire sustaining the hair next the first knot.
Sorti — A knot of ribbons to be seen between the pinner and the bonnet.
Flandan — A species of pinner joined to the bonnet.
Burgoigne — The frill nearest the hair.
Jardiné — The single pinner next the Burgoigne.
Cornett — The upper pinner dangling about the cheeks.

Besides all this, the Palisade, though not decorative, served its purpose as a wire frame for holding up all this absurd affair; the entire head-dress being called a Commode —which actually was a frame of wire, covered in silk, on which the head attire could be adjusted at once upon the head. The men's periwigs imitated the ladies' hairdressing in the two " horns " or curls directly over the forehead.

1690—1700

THE excessive ornamentation of ladies' attire may well be noticed on the example opposite. Gold braid and embroidery played a prominent part in decoration in the 'nineties. The sleeve, it will be observed, was no longer turned back into a cuff at the elbow, but often fell loose in a bell shape over the smock sleeve. The hair was often worn loose down the back, and especially by younger women, from about 1690.

In the example of men's attire it will be noticed that his cuffs are four deep. The excess of ribbons at this period was equal if not more than in earlier periods, though after 1692 only the scarlet bow was worn at the throat, the rest of the coat decoration relying on fur, braid, and embroidery. It should here be noticed how the cravat was wound around the neck and tied, hanging over the formal arrangement of ribbons. When untied, it was sometimes slipped through a button-hole on the coat, as illustrated on the next page.

The periwig no longer resembled the human hair, but was arranged in a mass of curls, those on the surface being cut at different lengths, to give the effect of ringlets all over. These locks were arranged in three or four separate bunches. Sometimes one mass behind and one over each shoulder, sometimes two at the back, as will be noticed on one of the previous pages—the back view of a gentleman in a black coat. The front of the wig was raised in two tufts over the temples, and the back of the head was left smooth to the nape of the neck, where the curls began.

Powder for the wig was introduced during the 'nineties, and although this method of hairdressing was not general for some years, there are many contemporary portraits of the periwig smothered in powder, and giving a greyish matted effect. A contemporary description of the youth who would be a gallant includes :

> " A powder'd Wig, a Sword, a page, a chair,
> Learn to take snuff, drink chocolate and swear."

1690—1700 (*continued*)

The bustle in its first form was introduced about 1690. The increasing tendency to bunch the skirts at the back during the 'eighties eventually resulted in a roll of padding round the back and sides of the petticoat, to give a yet wider silhouette. The bustle of the nineteenth century resembled that of the seventeenth century in many particulars: the tight-laced bodice and the frilled and ornamental petticoat was in some cases almost identical with that worn by our own mothers and grandmothers. Some of the Parisienne fashion-plates of this time might almost be those of the last century.

Ornament took on a formality similar to metal-work or iron-work, and the embroidered waistcoat worn by the ladies might almost have been a piece of armour so formal was it.

I have purposely omitted the waistcoat from the last figure on the opposite page, so that the knee-breeches may be seen. This type was first worn in the late 'eighties, and by about 1695 the fuller ones had ceased to exist. The skirt, it may be observed, was still full, with large sleeves and frills at the waist, the neck-line being brought right up to the throat and finished with a tiny band or frill. The cravat was often several yards in length, of silk, linen, or lace, and the ends always ornamented in some manner.

1690—1700 (*continued*)

In both examples of male attire on the opposite page, the long-sleeved waistcoat may be observed beneath the enormous cuff of the coat. The cuffs were more often than not well below the elbow after 1675. The first figure shows an exaggerated form of the curls over the temples. The ornate cuffs and pockets on this coat were decorated with black fur.

In Celia Fiennes' *Through England on Horseback*, there is an interesting description worthy of record of perhaps the earliest type of bathing suit: "The ladye goes into the bath with garments made of yellow canvas, which is stiff and made large with great sleeves like a parson's gown. The water fills it up so that it's borne off that your shape is not seen, it does not cling close as other lining." She goes on to say that the gentlemen wear drawers and waistcoats of the same sort of canvas. She also mentions in the same interesting, though monotonous, volume that Canterbury was a wonderful city with many French people, whose chief industry was silk-weaving. This silk-weaving must have been that alluded to at the beginning of this book.

Muffs and furs continued in favour during the 'nineties, the muffs usually being decorated with large bows of ribbon. The furs or palatines were always fastened with jewelled tags and clasps. The fashionable colour of fur included sable, ermine, and grey. Velvet scarves were often worn over the head-dress instead of the Rayonne.

1690—1700 (*continued*)

Every curl had its fashionable position and name. There were the Berger, Passague, Choux, Confidents, Cheve cœur, Cruches, and Frontange. The Berger was a plain small lock of hair turned up with a puff. The Passague was the curled lock at the temples. Confidets were the tiny curls near the ears. The Cheve cœur, or " heart-breakers," were the two small curled locks at the nape of the neck. Cruches were certain small curls on the forehead, and the Frontange was the top-knot—another fashion started by one of Louis XIV's mistresses—Madame Frontange.

❋ ❋ ❋

Here, then, is the rough outline of costume worn during the reigns of the romantic Stuarts—from Elizabeth to Anne—from farthingale to bustle—from high-piled hair to stilted informality in head-dressing. One may see the man—his Elizabethan doublet changing for the high-waisted square-tabbed French one, then the loose waistless jerkin, the jackanapes coat of a hundred ribbons, and then eventually evolving into the skirted coats and waistcoats of the eighteenth century. His hair is worn increasingly long, and eventually unsatisfied with nature's gifts he adorns his head with a monstrous periwig; this, in turn, elongating and becoming so large that no stretch of imagination could recognize it as a head of human hair. Foot-wear develops from a soft, slashed satin shoe, decorated with a satin rosette, to a ridiculously fantastic boot, cut, lined, and decorated to a point of absurdity, until it becomes a stiff, long, square-toed leather shoe, with a large lined flap over the instep, and decorated with buckles instead of ribbons. Breeches pass through numerous phases from the bombasted gathered stockings called farthingales by James I, to the tight-fitting knee-breeches of the eighteenth century; taking in their stride the odd petticoat-breeches of the 'forties and 'sixties, the laced and ribboned affair of the Cavalier, the ugly plus-four-like calf-length breeches of the Roundhead fraternity, and the curious baggy, almost ankle-length frills of the late 'sixties.

And so we reach the end of a century full of new ideas, and holding far more variety in masculine attire than any other hundred years.

English Costume of the Eighteenth Century

FOREWORD

THE phrase " eighteenth-century costume " is one dear to theatrical costumiers, and (although there has been a very considerable diffusion of knowledge during the last few years) it is still too often used as though the same clothes were worn from 1700 to 1800. Eighteenth-century plays are frequently dressed quite regardless of changes in fashion throughout the century. Ramillies wigs are wedded to 1790 hats ; Louis XV. petticoats are worn with the towering head-dresses of 1770, and Watteau gowns are matched with *toilettes* of the French Directory.

That there is some excuse for this the following pages bear witness. There is indeed a singular homogeneity about the period, and when one considers that fashions came in and went out more slowly than they do at present, that the difference between town and country was more marked, and that old people clung more affectionately to the modes of their youth, there is perhaps less absurdity in treating the century as one than might at first appear.

The present editor would be the last person to advocate a pedantic archæological accuracy in reconstructing the costume and background of the Comedy of Manners. There is a sense in which the eighteenth century—if we forget the revolutionary fervour of its close—was static, as timeless and changeless as a Platonic Idea. The three-cornered hat, the Watteau gown, the wig, the snuff-box, the shoe-buckles, the knee-breeches, and the sword at a man's side—these are surely Types laid up in Heaven.

The sixteenth century had been convulsed by the Reformation, the seventeenth by the Wars of Religion ; all was confusion, all was flux. But in the eighteenth century the surface of civilisation seemed to have set hard ; a culture had been evolved which, however incapable of satisfying the eternal needs of man, was, of its kind, perfect and complete.

That is not to say that it had no hidden misery and horror, no filth, no squalor, no sordid poverty. It had all these things; but it had also a Society, in the true sense, a European Society conscious of its unity and its common culture, and able therefore to devote itself to the elaboration of the elegancies of life, in a word to the evolution of Style. In nearly all the countries of Europe, Aristocracy had come to terms with Monarchy and had not yet been overwhelmed by the democratic flood. *Après nous, le déluge!* But till it came, the polite world enjoyed itself, and has left to future ages a complete picture of a homogeneous culture, a culture in which formal religion was tempered by scepticism and extravagance was restrained by taste, and in which two arts at least were brought to their perfection: the art of letter-writing and the art of conversation.

The calm was, of course, delusive, the seemingly solid surface scored with fissures and threatened with subterranean upheaval. Every age, no matter how static it may appear, is an age of transition, and the eighteenth century was no exception. Thought changed and fashion with it, and the century which began with Addison ended by accepting the extravagances of Rousseau. Costume is not a triviality; it is the visible raiment of the soul. It is the purpose of the present book to display the slow but, in the end, considerable changes which affected European costume during the eighteenth century.

1700

1700—1705

THE beginning of the century found the dress of Charles II.'s last years only slightly modified by the intervening reigns. James introduced no innovations, and the slight Dutch influence due to William III. only served to give to dress a certain stiffness and sombreness in keeping with the temperament of a King who cared nothing for the elegancies of life. Queen Anne, with whom the century opened, brought neither gaiety nor ostentation to a Court singularly lacking in both, and the dress of her period followed the rigid form of her predecessors. The main lines of costume, however, as it was to exist for nearly a century, were already decided, and this costume had certain strong characteristics which must be briefly considered.

The most remarkable of such characteristics is the wig. Wigs were worn in France very early in the seventeenth century, but did not reach England until the Restoration. Charles II. wore a voluminous black wig, and throughout his reign the wig fell on each side of the face with the ends drooping on to the chest. This proved so inconvenient, especially for soldiers, that the fashion arose of tying the hair back with a ribbon, and ultimately, of enclosing it at the back in a silk bag. But this, at the opening of the century, was still in the future. The cost of wigs was enormous, as much as £30 being frequently paid for a full wig of real hair. When one considers that this must have been the equivalent of at least £100 of our money, it is not surprising that foot-pads should make a first snatch at their victims' wigs.

Men's coats were so long that they almost concealed the breeches, and the waistcoats were almost as long as the coats. Shoe-buckles came in with William III., and were at first very small. They soon grew larger, and were often ornamented with jewels.

Women's dress was somewhat severe, although it had certain elements of informality. The small laced apron was much worn, even on important occasions. Below it was the flowered petticoat, much more important than the skirt, which was frequently drawn back in bunches or folds. The bodice of the dress, although cut low, was very stiff.

1705—1710

THE most striking thing about female costume at the beginning of the eighteenth century was the height of the head-dress. The fashion started in France when Mademoiselle Fontange, the King's mistress, finding her hair disordered while out hunting, tied it up with a ribbon. The fashion was followed, and formalised, so that soon an elaborate high lace cap stood on the women's heads, the hair being piled up in front and adorned with a wire frame covered with lace and ribbons. The Fontange head-dress was called a " commode " in England, and was seen as early as the end of James II.'s reign. It lasted throughout the reign of William and Mary, and, at the accession of Queen Anne, rose even higher. The lace used was very costly, for there was as yet no substitute for the real lace of Brussels and Mechlin except gauze, which did not give the same effect. Men's hair was cropped very close, and in private the heavy full-bottomed wig was frequently discarded, an embroidered cap being worn in its place. Poets and painters are frequently represented in this curious negligé Waistcoats were still excessively long, and had to be left unbuttoned at the bottom in order to allow freedom to the limbs. Shirts were made of fine white lawn, with elaborate lace frills down the front and at the wrists. The cravat, which was also of lace, was one of the most costly parts of the costume. The sword was, of course, worn by all gentlemen, and had not yet assumed the dainty proportions of the dress-sword later in the century—a sword of the same size and shape as that which survives to-day in Court dress. Small boys did not wear a wig, but kept their own hair long in a kind of curly mop.

1700—1710

THE neckcloth, or cravat, had been worn by German troops as early as 1640, and, soon after the beginning of the new century, began to replace the lace collar in general use. It consisted of a strip of white material about a foot wide and a yard long, twisted round the neck and knotted in front. Considerable variety was practised in the manner of tying it, and each variety had a special name. A Steinkerk was a lace cravat tied very loosely, with the ends passed through a buttonhole in the coat. It was so called after the Battle of Steinkerk, where the French officers went into action so hurriedly that they had not time to tie their cravats properly; and the fashion was popular in England in spite of the fact that Steinkerk was an English defeat.

The large wig was worn by the wealthy, unconfined by any kind of ribbon or fastening, a fashion which must have been extremely inconvenient for those whose occupations involved rapid physical action.

The very short sleeve of Charles II.'s time had given place to a longer variety, with very elaborate turned-back cuffs, adorned with buttons and embroidery. Women's sleeves remained almost the same for many years. They were short, reaching to just below the elbow, and were finished with rather wide lace ruffles. Sometimes the lace was attached to the chemisette underneath, and not to the gown itself.

The odd habit of wearing patches on the face lasted almost throughout the century, and patches of different shapes and sizes were worn by women of all ages. Painting the face was freely indulged in, and the paints used sometimes contained chemicals very harmful to the complexion. The face was treated with wash-balls compounded of white lead, rice, and flour, with washes of quicksilver boiled in water, and with bismuth. This mattered less, perhaps, because women expected to look old in the early 'thirties.

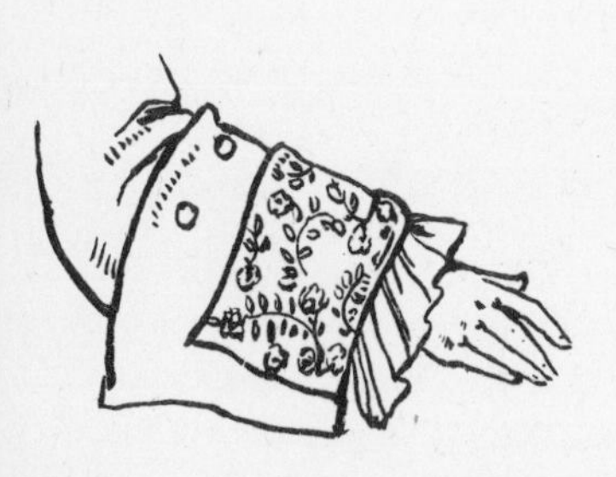

1710

THERE is no very noticeable change in men's attire during the first ten years of the eighteenth century. Coats and waistcoats remained very long with large pockets in the flaps of each. The stockings were worn outside the breeches, drawn up over the knee, but gartered below. Stockings could be of coloured silk—blue or scarlet—with gold or silver clocks, but youths and poorer men wore black stockings of wool. In winter the curious fashion was followed of wearing several pairs of stockings at once.

In women's dress the fashions of the end of the previous century had been but slightly modified. The corset, which had reappeared about 1670, was worn very tight, and the bodice of the over-dress cut to fit exactly over it. It was laced from the bottom, with the effect of forcing the breasts upwards. Bodices were low, and a crimped frill was added to the upper edge—a survival from the lace collar of the previous age.

Already before the close of the seventeenth century gowns began to be looped up at the sides into *paniers*, and these *paniers* were superseded by hoops, which soon grew to enormous dimensions. The hoop was not, like the crinoline, an under-garment, but the outside petticoat itself stiffened with whalebone. The over-gown opened in front, and the petticoat was frequently of damask or other rich cloth. In winter petticoats were sometimes made of ermine, but, as by their nature, they were some little distance from the body of the wearer, they could not have made her much warmer. Petticoat, gown, stays, and cloak could be of different colours, but it was the petticoat which was usually embroidered and therefore formed the richest part of the toilet.

1710—1720

In its earliest and most elaborate form the full-bottomed wig was divided into three masses of curls, two in front of the shoulders and one hanging down the back. Above the forehead the hair rose into two peaks or horns, sometimes exaggerated to grotesque proportions. However, the fashion served to give increased height to the figure, and a grave dignity to the face. A hat was completely unnecessary, and was often carried in the hand, but when worn, had to be of considerable size. The back of the head was smooth, the artificial curls forming a fringe at the edge of the wig.

The hoop petticoat made its first appearance in the London streets in 1711, and two English ladies, walking in the gardens of the Tuileries in 1718, set the fashion in France. It has been suggested that it came from Germany, from some little Court where the great wheel farthingale known to Queen Elizabeth and to Anne of Denmark had survived for more than a century. The revived hoop was at its biggest in England at the end of the other Queen Anne's reign.

The skirts of a man's coat were stiffened with wire to make them stand out, but men soon abandoned the attempt to compete with their wives in this particular.

Falbalas came in early in the century. These were crimped or pleated flounces sewn horizontally round the skirt, and were sometimes of a different material. This was not true of *volants* or wide ruffles, which were assumed to be part of the original dress.

The English corset was in general laced at the back, and the whalebone stiffening went right round the body and across the breast. The top edge was stiffened with a stout wire, and in the lining in front a small pocket was contrived to hold satchets of fragrant herbs. The French corset continued to be laced up the front.

1715

IT is often assumed that dress in the eighteenth century was very much more formal than it is to-day. In reality it was much less so, in the sense that considerably greater variety was permitted to individual taste, and that costume had not yet crystallised, as it were, into various accepted forms for different occasions and different occupations. An eighteenth-century gentleman would have been astonished at the uniformity of men's evening-dress, and even at the comparative uniformity of their everyday attire. Pages were not yet dressed in buttons, nor Eton boys in short coats and white collars. If lawyers wore full-bottomed wigs, so did every other dignified man. Lackeys wore the costume of the day with certain modifications; there was even a certain amount of liberty allowed in officers' uniforms, and a definitely naval costume had not yet been invented. In particular, Court dress was simply the dress of the day, a little more elaborate and a little more costly.

Immense numbers of diamonds were worn both by men and women, for since the Dutch improvements in diamond-cutting at the beginning of the century, the stones could be made to present a much more brilliant effect than formerly. Diamonds were often borrowed or even hired for important occasions, such as Courts and weddings. The somewhat rigid bodice-fronts of this period lent themselves to the display of precious stones, and the stomacher was frequently embroidered all over with them, or else heavily laced with gold thread. Peers and Knights of the Garter and other orders wore their decorations even in the street, so that a man's rank could be easily recognised. We are still far from the days when it is considered bad form to wear even a miniature military ribbon. In this sense the dress of the eighteenth century was very formal; and although the middle classes tried to ape the nobility, the high cost of the materials worn compelled them to keep at a respectful distance.

1710—1720

THE fashion for wearing the full-bottomed wig divided into three masses of curls did not last very long, owing to the growing consciousness of its inconvenience, even among the leisured. Later, the wig was of equal length all round, but sometimes the portion at the back was divided into two, the ends being tied with ribbons. This fashion persisted among old men until about 1760, but in general wigs became smaller about 1720, and continued to diminish in size throughout the century.

Cuffs were still large and sometimes heavily embroidered, but disappeared from hunting and riding coats. Riding was also responsible for a modification of the coat-tails. These were buttoned back, and soon became merely ornamental, *i.e.* the revers were formalised as part of the decoration of the coat, thus making the wider opening at the front of the coat permanent. The last vestige of this buttoning back is to be seen in the two black buttons in the small of the back of a modern morning or evening coat and in the more elaborate arrangement of buttons on the back lower edge of a soldier's tunic.

The most notable change in female attire is a lowering of the head-dress. On the disappearance of the " commode " or Fontange head-dress, the hair was worn in a simple, almost negligent style, rather close to the head. This fashion lasted, with but slight modifications, until the introduction of the towering head-dresses typical of the seventeen-seventies. The habit of wearing caps, however, persisted, particularly in the middle classes. These caps were usually quite small and perched on the top of the head, but were sometimes very rich, trimmed with fine lace, or made of lace entirely. Servants' caps, or the caps worn by very old ladies and peasant women, are now the only survivals of this practice.

1720

AT the beginning of the century the increased facilities for trade with the East, due to the growing success of the East India Company, led to the introduction of vast quantities of Indian calicoes, which soon became very popular. English cloth manufacturers grew alarmed, and Acts of Parliament were passed, both by Queen Anne and George I., prohibiting the use of calicoes, silks, etc., from India, Persia, and China. These were, however, extensively smuggled, and Steele, in his plea for the weavers of England, gives an interesting list of the materials they had displaced : brilliants, pulerays, antherines, bombazines, satinets, chiverets, oraguellas, grazetts (flowered and plain), footworks, coloured crapes (although most crape was made in Italy and was regarded by rigid Protestants as Popish), damasks, and worsted tammy draughts.

A wide over-dress came into fashion about this period. It hung loose from the shoulders and could be fastened down the front with bows of ribbon. This, which was called a *contouche*, was the equivalent of the modern *peignoir*, and at first was worn only in the house as a morning-dress, but soon became so popular that it appeared everywhere in the street. It could be made of silk, wool, or taffeta and sometimes of light materials, such as gauze or muslin, worn over an under-dress of a contrasting colour. Its effect was one of charming negligence in attire, and is typical of the change which was taking place, less noticeably in England than in France, from the stiff formalism of the age of Louis XIV. to the rather frivolous elegance of the Rococo period. Men's coats were still rather sombre in hue, embroidery being reserved for the decoration of the waistcoat, which was often the most valuable part of the costume, unless the lace ruffles of the shirt were exceptionally fine.

1720—1725

THE seventeen-twenties were marked by the increasing popularity of the *contouche*, already described. It must not be thought, however, that the wearing of one of these loose dresses meant the abandonment of corsets. These formed an essential part of the under-dress, and were still worn very tightly laced in order to give a small waist to the figure, even when this was completely hidden by the full *contouche*.

Until about the year 1725, men wore on the right shoulders of their coats a number of bows of ribbon, the long ends of which extended to the elbows. These were a relic of the shoulder fastening which had been used at the end of the seventeenth century to secure the sword belt. Swords were now worn less conspicuously and sometimes discarded altogether except on formal occasions or for going about London by night, when the unarmed pedestrian was at the mercy of footpads and riotous marauders of all kinds. It was usual, therefore, to go to evening entertainments in the company of friends or servants.

Heel-making was a separate trade, employing a large number of hands, and this fact no doubt contributed to the persistence of high heels. The heels even of men's shoes were in general high, those of women extremely so. They were made of wood and coloured. In France, red heels were a sign of noble birth. The shape of shoes in general, even women's shoes, was somewhat clumsy, the heels being far too small and placed too near the middle of the instep. It would have been impossible to walk far in such shoes, and in the house women wore slippers.

For out of doors, ladies wore a long cloak with a hood attached to it. It was originally of scarlet cloth, and perhaps for that reason was called a "cardinal." It remained scarlet until the close of the century, when it became the fashion to wear black cloaks. It is interesting to note that the "cardinal" was the cloak worn by "Little Red Riding Hood" in the nursery story.

1725—1730

TRAVELLING cloaks for men were long and circular in shape, in fact they differed little from the *chlamys* of the Greeks (except that this was oblong), or the cloaks worn by Spanish peasants to this day. The appalling state of the roads in wet weather made high, stout boots essential, and these were of the pattern familiar from pictures of the Restoration period but with narrower tops, and, of course, unadorned with lace round the upper edge. For riding and travelling, women wore a modification of the male coat with turned-back sleeves and cravat, but their skirts were ill-adapted for any kind of exercise.

By 1730 the re-introduced farthingale may be said to have established itself, to last, with slight modifications, until the French Revolution. It grew to six feet in diameter and required an enormous quantity of stuff to cover it. At first, hoops of osier rods or cane were used, but these were superseded by the more reliable whalebone. The hoop was at first simply a cage—a series of hoops of different dimensions attached to one another by ribbons or strings at intervals round their circumference. About 1729 it became customary to cover this cage with cloth, with taffeta, and finally with silk, so that the hoop became a reinforced skirt. Sometimes in summer no other skirt was worn, and as the wearing of drawers was still very uncommon, the limbs were naked underneath the hoop except for the stockings which reached to just above the knee and were fastened by garters just below it. Hoops were violently denounced from the pulpit, but from any contest with the clergy fashion has always emerged victorious, and they continued to be worn even by servant girls, and by countrywomen going to market. Even the simplest *négligé* was duly provided with its framework of whalebone, and it became impossible for two women to walk abreast in the narrow streets or to occupy a carriage together in comfort. Even the staircases in private houses had to be provided with balusters curved outward in order to allow for the passage of the voluminous skirts.

1720—1730

BAG-WIGS were at first worn chiefly by soldiers, and when they made their way into civilian costume were regarded, in the beginning, as a kind of undress. The bag was made of gummed black taffeta, with a bow of the same material, and served to give an appearance of neatness without much trouble. The pig-tail was almost as popular as the bag-wig and for the same reasons of convenience. The *toupet*, or hair immediately over the forehead, was often natural, the join between the wig and the real hair being disguised by a liberal use of powder.

About 1730 the fashion arose of leaving the top buttons of the waistcoat unfastened in order to display the elaborately frilled shirt. This led to a modification of the neckcloth, which had shorter ends in order that the decorated shirt-front might be more easily seen. Sometimes the cravat with shorter ends was replaced by a neckcloth knotted at the back and kept in place in front by a jewelled pin. Military men wore two neckcloths one over the other, the under one of white muslin and that over it of coloured silk, allowing the white of the first to show between the folds.

Throughout the century, women's sleeves were almost constant in length, that is to say, the material of the dress reached just to the point of the elbow, and further length was given by two or three frills of lace. Although the elaborate "commode" had disappeared, smaller caps of lace were still worn in the house by women of all ranks and all ages. The styles of hairdressing varied considerably but within narrow limits, the hair being kept fairly close to the head. The necks of dresses were worn very low, in fact as low as a modern evening-dress, except that the opening was not so deep at the back.

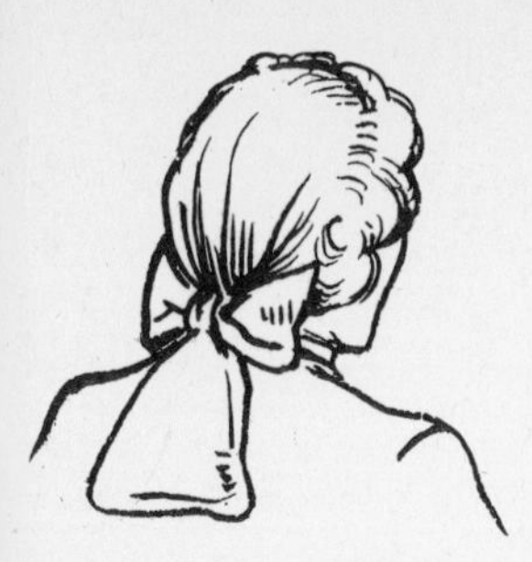

1730

THE three-cornered hat, than which nothing is more typical of eighteenth-century fashion, was capable of a considerable amount of variety. Some hats were still laced and garnished with plumes like those of the previous epoch, but as the plume was worn on the upper brim, now bent inwards, it only appeared as a kind of fringe. Some hats were simply bordered with braid. The triangular form was kept by means of a cord, passed through holes in the brim and drawn tight round the crown, or else by a button acting as a kind of clip at the edge of the upturned brim. The earlier habit of festooning the hat with ribbons h ad been definitely abandoned.

The accession of George II. made very little difference to costume in England. The new king, like the old, was German, stiff in his manners and somewhat slovenly in his habits. His Court provided no centre of influence for the caprices of Society or the whims of fashion. Individual members of the aristocracy wielded far more influence than the Royal Family, and those who could afford trips to the Continent became, by natural consequence, the arbiters of taste.

Two accessories of costume in constant use were the snuff-box and the fan. The first was carried by every man, of every degree, and by many ladies. The smoking of tobacco was considered definitely "low," to be practised only by sailors and labourers, but vast quantities of the weed were consumed in the form of snuff powder, and every elegance of decoration was bestowed upon the boxes in which it was carried.

The fan was universal. In Queen Anne's reign it had been very large. Later, it became less pretentious and was decorated with painted scenes by the most able artists. Sometimes the paintings were designed to show political opinions. The material used was paper or, sometimes, thin white chicken skin, and the handles could be ornamented with jewels or enamels.

1730—1735

IN 1734 women's stays were worn extremely low. The bodies of gowns were laced up the front over a stomacher, or else stays were worn outside ; but in general there is little change in feminine costume since the last decade.

Men's costume also remained almost static, although the bag-wig was steadily ousting more elaborate types of coiffure. The turned back cuffs, frequently of contrasting colour to that of the coat, were cut in " pagoda " fashion, that is to say, narrow at the wrist and expanding sharply along the forearm. The name is a sufficient indication of the slight Oriental influence which made itself felt throughout the eighteenth century, not, however, so much affecting the shape of clothes as their colour, material, and decoration.

In France about 1730 men began to fasten their breeches at the knee over the stockings, but the older mode persisted among Englishmen for some years longer. The winter of 1729 was one of exceptional severity, and fine gentlemen, finding their thin stockings an insufficient protection against the cold, wore for a few months a kind of military gaiter. Men of the lower classes, with their grey or black woollen stockings, were better protected and had no need to adopt this short-lived fashion.

The fashion of leaving the waistcoat open in front in order to display the linen has been already mentioned. The custom reached its extreme in the early 'thirties. Sometimes, about a foot of frilled shirt was shown—a fashion to which the modern dress shirt and low-cut waistcoat can be ultimately traced. Women's riding-habits affected, as so often, a masculine mode, the waistcoat being shorter but of the same pattern, and the hat smaller but similar in shape to those worn by men.

Men's pockets were very ample and the folds of the long coat made it possible to carry comparatively bulky objects in them without spoiling their shape. Some fashionable gentlemen would carry a whole battery of snuff-boxes in the skirts of their coats.

1735—1740

THE arrival of Queen Caroline in England (for previously the Royal Court had remained in Hanover) gave a certain impulse to fashion, which had for some time languished without a leader. The Queen of George II. had a great liking for flowered silks, usually with a white ground embossed all over with a large pattern of gold, silver, or colours.

George II. himself had no pretensions to be a leader of fashion. His tastes were those of a simple soldier, and he had no feeling for any of the elegances of life. The ladies he honoured with his favour were neither beautiful nor elegant, and the English aristocracy went its own way, independent of the Court, adopting French fashions to its own slightly more rural use, but inventing little of its own. The prestige which English costume was to exercise all over the Continent was still more than half a century in the future.

Women of the middle classes still dressed with a certain austerity, although the wives and daughters of rich City merchants did their best to copy the fashions of St. James's. Some of the merchants themselves assumed, on Sundays, the fine coats and elaborate periwigs of the nobility.

Women's stockings, until the middle of the seventeen-thirties, were of all colours, green being one of the favourites. They were worked with clocks of gold, silver, or coloured silks. About 1737, however, there was a sudden rage for white stockings which greatly alarmed contemporary moralists. White stockings seemed to the preachers little better than nudity, but they continued to be worn until almost the end of the century. As a matter of fact very little of the stocking was seen, as dresses were never shorter in this period than to just above the ankles. Dancing or climbing into a coach may have revealed a certain amount of stocking to the eyes of the curious, but not enough, one would have thought, to alarm the most rigorous censor of morals.

1730—1740

IN addition to tie-wigs of many varieties there appeared, in the reign of George II., bob-wigs of various kinds. These imitated natural hair much more closely than the grand peruques; they were worn by professional men, citizens, and even by apprentices; lawyers affected a high frontlet and a long bag at the back tied in the middle, undergraduates a wig with a flat top to allow for the academic cap.

Cravats in this period show very few modifications; in fact, although there were many varieties, each variety was almost as static as the modern neck-tie. The fronts and cuffs of shirts continued to be elaborately frilled. Coat-cuffs were wide and deep and sometimes heavily embroidered with silk flowers or with patterns in gold and silver thread.

There is little change to record in the forms of women's head-dresses. The ideal of the small, neat head was maintained; caps became even smaller than they had been, and curls more neatly trimmed and arranged. The general shape of the female figure continued to be an equilateral triangle, resting securely on a wide base. The lower part of the body was inside the skirt rather than clothed by it, the only underclothes worn being in the form of a long "smock" or chemise. The evolution of underclothes should form an interesting and necessary chapter in the history of fashion. The phrase "body-linen" is still sometimes used, but actual linen underclothes must now be extremely rare. In the eighteenth century, however, linen was the usual material, very fine Dutch linen being imported for ladies' "smocks." Scotch or Irish linen could be bought for a third of the price, but was coarser and not so highly esteemed. Silk and lace-trimmed underwear was unknown in the eighteenth century.

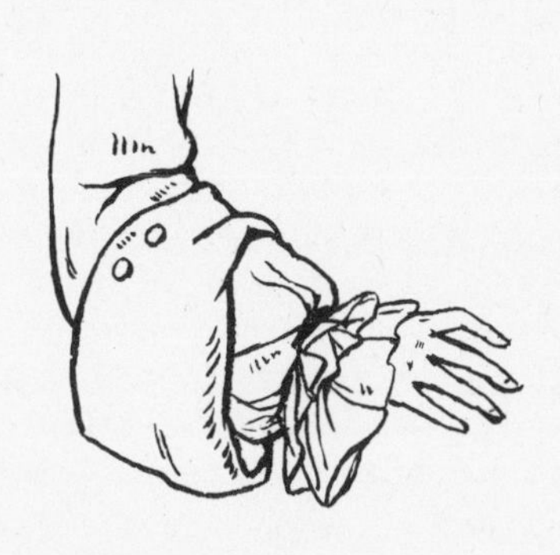

1740

THE inconvenience of the circular hoop led to the introduction of one oval in shape, and much more graceful in appearance. The materials, although not so heavy as the brocades used early in the century, were very rich, and often extremely costly.

An ingenious method was evolved (or rather revived from the Elizabethan and Caroline periods) for decorating women's dresses. This was the process of quilting which had the added advantage, in winter, of making the clothes much warmer. A layer of wadding was spread between the lining (which had to be of linen or some equally strong material) and the material of the dress, and was kept in place by an elaborate stitchery pattern. Another method of decoration was to cut out shapes of the same material as the dress and to sew them on to it, having first inserted a stuffing of wadding. These were known as " plastic ornaments."

As the century advanced, and the general prosperity increased, there was a gradual filtering down of luxury from the aristocracy to the upper middle-classes. Working people, especially in the large towns, often lived under conditions which would not now be tolerated, but the general standard of life rose steadily, until the set-back of the Industrial Revolution.

The fine ladies of the period vied in extravagance with their sisters on the other side of the Channel, and like them adopted certain exotic modes intended to give them an air of elegant eccentricity. The possession of a monkey or a green parrot was a sign of luxurious refinement, and those who could afford it went even further and purchased a little black boy as a personal attendant. The presence of such a slave, dressed in bright coloured and fantastic clothes, was eminently calculated to set off both the toilette and the white skin of his mistress.

1740—1745

IT should not be forgotten, in considering the costumes of a period as remote from us as the eighteenth century, that the tyranny of fashion was nothing like so complete as it is at present. Perhaps it would be truer to say that although fashion was tyrannical it was much less swift in its operation and, in the absence of fashion plates, a change in dress took much longer to filter down through the different strata of society. People in the country might well be twenty years behind the fashion, and the older men and women, even in towns, sometimes did not trouble to adjust themselves to changing taste.

In 1740, for example, it was quite possible to see an oldish man walking, even in the fashionable St. James's Park, in a large full-bottomed wig, while his son beside him wore one much smaller and neater. Older men clung also to their old-fashioned cravats, just as older men to-day wear the collars which were usual in their youth. There is perhaps no article of a man's attire about which he seems so conservative as his neckwear.

Women's dress shows certain modifications which must be briefly noted. The *sacque* gown, hanging loose from the shoulders and gathered in great folds over the hooped petticoat, appeared in 1740. It was another example of the general tendency to exalt the *négligé* into general wear. The effect could be charming, but involved considerable skill in dressmaking. Examination of the actual dresses of the period reveals the delicate cutting which was necessary in order to give the loose appearance at the back and yet mould the dress to the figure, for the falling folds were not added afterwards like a cape, but were an essential part of the back of the bodice.

1745—1750

THE loose *contouche*, already described, went out of fashion at the end of the seventeen-forties. Instead, there was introduced a gown or *robe ronde*, which opened from the waist downwards to display an underdress of the same material. In morning attire the place of the *contouche* was taken by various kinds of powder-mantles or dressing-jackets. The practice of powdering the hair demanded some kind of protection for the dress while the operation was being performed, and the toilette of a fashionable lady took up so much of her time and was attended, as a kind of informal reception, by so many of her friends (particularly men), that some kind of garment was necessary which was both warm and becoming. A woman of fashion was surrounded, from the moment she got out of bed, by a crowd of admirers, dressmakers, furniture vendors, musicians, dancing-masters, and dependents. Such a miniature court can be studied in all its detail in the well-known engraving by Hogarth.

Women's shoes were excessively flimsy and ill-adapted to any kind of hard wear. This fact receives interesting confirmation from a document, found among Lady Suffolk's papers, which gives details of the dress allowances for the daughters of George II. The provision was not on the whole extravagant, twelve pairs of thread stockings and two dozen cambric pocket-handkerchiefs being expected to last for two years, but a new pair of shoes, at six shillings a pair, was provided every week. Nine " day shifts " and nine " night shifts " were given to the princesses yearly, but the allowance of gloves rose to the astonishing annual figure of sixteen dozen pairs. It must be remembered, however, that in Royal households servants rapidly acquire a right to certain perquisites, and that articles of clothing were given away long before they were worn out. It was enacted, however, that the fine lace trimmings on the princesses' garments were not to be given away but saved for future use.

1740—1750

IN the early 'forties of the eighteenth century wigs became somewhat smaller, sometimes not touching the shoulders at all. By dandies they were sometimes worn exceedingly small, although satirical prints of the period probably overstressed their minuteness. The hat became smaller also, with very little border turned up to make the three-cornered shape. Cravats were smaller, and as this exposed more of the shirt, the front of this was more extravagantly frilled. The turned-down collar of the coat made an occasional appearance, as if in anticipation of the fashions at the end of the century, but this was unusual in the 'forties. Cuffs were still large but tended to be somewhat narrower at the wrist. Later in the decade hats were larger again, but wigs remained small, a contrast which had the effect of making the hat seem larger still.

Women still wore their hair somewhat close to the head, with one or two curls falling behind and others encircling the face. Caps were universally worn, sometimes approximating in shape to those worn by Mary, Queen of Scots, a lady to whom fashion has more than once returned for fresh inspiration. " Milkmaid " fashions for women had already made their appearance, and these involved country hats tied negligently under the chin with ribbons. Such hats are the remote ancestors of the nineteenth-century poke-bonnet. Throughout the eighteenth century colours had a political significance, and it is interesting to note that white hat-ribbons at this period denoted Jacobite sympathies. It is not always realised how much sympathy there was in England in 1745 for the attempt of the Young Pretender on the throne of his ancestors. If he had succeeded, the formalising influence of a German Court would have been removed, and English fashions would have been rapidly assimilated to those of the French, as had happened once before on the Restoration of another Charles Stuart.

1750

THE middle of the century marked what is perhaps the highest point of rococo style. The stiffness of the earlier years had been abandoned, and the extravagances of the 'seventies and the neo-classical negligence of the 'nineties were alike unthought of. The most typical characteristics of the century were at their most charming stage. The wig was neat and becoming. The three-cornered hat was of medium size—it had been ridiculously large in Marlborough's time, and became ridiculously small in 1790 ; coats and waistcoats were both dignified and graceful, the cut was good and the embroidery elegant. There was a tasteful moderation in the use of lace.

Women's dress was marked by a peculiarly charming form of the side *panier*, and was made of bright stuffs not too rich and heavy, for one result of the large *panier* had been to lead to the introduction of lighter and more flexible materials for dresses. In the late seventeenth and early eighteenth centuries very heavy stuffs had been worn, as these lent themselves to the somewhat rigid silhouettes of fashionable costume. The feminine frame, while capable of much in deference to fashion, cannot support an unlimited quantity of heavy brocade interwoven with metal strands. Some women managed to support damask, which is a heavy material, but looked well, with its bold patterns, when stretched over hoops ; but for the majority the result of the new modes was the introduction of lawn, muslin, and dimity, of simple texture but lively pattern, little bouquets or scattered flowers being the most frequent. The universal crinoline of a century later was to have a very similar effect.

1750—1755

THE year 1750 witnessed a striking decrease in the size of hoops, but the fashion for widening the skirt by the artificial aid of whalebone or osier rods was not to be abandoned for another generation, and in Court dress for another sixty years. The persistence and recurrence of hoops is one of the oddest phenomena in the history of fashion, and it is by no means absolutely certain, even yet, that they will not return. In 1800 it may well have seemed that they had gone for ever, but they had assumed their most extravagant form again in 1860, and that in the middle of the triumphs of the machine age, when the necessity of getting in and out of railway carriages might well seem to have made their use impossible.

Tight-lacing also, prevalent in 1750, was equally so a century later, and may come in again unless it is defeated by the modern enthusiasm for sport. Although it is always dangerous to generalise in questions of fashion, it may be said that tight-lacing is never very far away when the waist-line is normal. The only way to be certain of abolishing the corset is to push the waistline to just below the breasts, as was done during the first decade of the nineteenth century, or to lower it to the hips, as was the fashion about 1928.

The fullness of women's dresses during the early seventeen-fifties was reflected in the fullness of the skirts of men's coats. These, too, were sometimes stiffened with whale-bone, or at least kept in place by pads, an odd example of the rare influence of feminine on masculine modes, since no man wishes to give the appearance of having full hips. In general, masculine fashions influence those of women far more frequently than feminine fashions influence those of men.

1755—1760

CONTRARY to the fashion at the beginning of the century, men's suits were sometimes made of the same elaborately patterned material throughout. This could be a cut velvet or an embroidered silk, and was naturally costly. The silk embroidery on men's coats sometimes involved months or even years of labour on the part of embroideresses, whose skill and taste have never been surpassed. Embroidered waistcoats were often the work of a man's wife or daughters, and making them served to pass the long winter evenings in an age almost devoid of outside entertainment.

Women's dresses were also sometimes embroidered, but relied more often on a woven pattern, or on tucks and flounces in the material itself. In the actual form of dress there was very little change, and in England at least, in the last few years of the reign of George II., there was no very outstanding example of feminine elegance to give a lead to fashion. What tendency may be traced was rather in the direction of simplicity, or what passed for such in an essentially artificial age when women took no exercise beyond a quiet stroll. Some gowns affected an air of elegant negligence by having neither bodice nor girdle, but hanging loose from the shoulders over the wide *panier*; others were fitted to the figure in front, but hung loose at the back. For this fashion heavy stuffs were unsuitable, so that dresses came to be made of lighter fabrics, such as lawn, muslin, or dimity, sometimes richly patterned, a tendency already noted as being due, in part, to the width of the hoops. The delicacy of the materials of dresses made some kind of protection from the weather doubly necessary. Cloaks with hoods were worn, and the sedan chair, for those who could afford it, saved the shoes of the ladies from being spoilt by the appallingly muddy streets. It is worthy of note that the umbrella first made its appearance in the London streets in 1756. It was carried by the philanthropist, Jonas Hanway, but his example was not generally followed for many years.

1750—1760

THE seventeen-fifties were a period of great importance in English history, and it is strange that the enormous military activity of the decade all over the world should have had so little effect even upon masculine fashions. The explanation, no doubt, lies partly in the fact that British victories took place for the most part in distant lands—at Plassey and at Quebec. Even the wars in Germany must have seemed sufficiently remote in that slow-travelling century, and although London swarmed with military men, especially in winter when the armies went into quarters, male fashion reflected the prevailing martial atmosphere only so far as to simplify the wig a little or give a military cock to the three-cornered hat.

On feminine costume the wars, unlike those of the Napoleonic era, left almost no trace at all, for the fashions were essentially feminine and so less susceptible than the revolutionary modes of the end of the century. It must also be remembered that the dress of soldiers was much closer in cut to that of civilians than during the days of the French Empire, when the fancy of military tailors was given full scope and the cut of uniforms decided for more than a century. Soldiers, in general, wore the civilian three-cornered hat, except that it was braided in a special way. Only grenadiers wore the mitre cap, and this was unlikely to be adopted for ordinary attire. The prevailing colour of British uniforms was already red, but the coats of civilians were frequently red also, and could be any colour. An officer was recognisable as such, but was by no means so conspicuous a figure in an ordinary crowd as a guardsman in full uniform would be to-day.

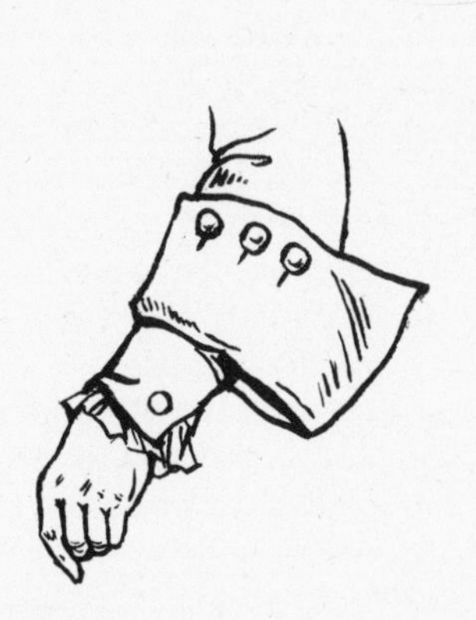

1760

AT the accession of George III., costume was, on the whole, simple, and the staid example of the Court did not tend to extravagance in dress. Hoops were still in use, but were of more reasonable size than had been fashionable a few years earlier. The small " gypsy hat " was worn even by the nobility. The gown was long-waisted and laced over the stomacher. Sleeves reached to the elbow, but full ruffles made them seem longer. Lace, in fact, was the chief extravagance, even the apron being frequently garnished with it. Handkerchiefs were frequently very costly, and more attention was paid to underclothes than during previous periods. Stockings were often white and made of silk and were fastened by garters, in general tied below the knee. Suspenders were, of course, impossible, as there was nothing to attach them to.

A *coqueluchon*, or small cape, covered the shoulders—a very necessary protection in cold weather, as bodices were somewhat low. Indeed, the high-necked bodice, even for day wear, is unusual until well on into the nineteenth century.

Children's costume, as such, had not yet been evolved, and boys and girls wore, with slight modification, replicas of their parents' clothes. Little girls, by modern standards, were far too heavily clad, and active boys were encumbered with long coats and three-cornered hats. In general, however, the costume of children showed, even as early as 1760, a tendency to simplicity and an adaptation to country usages, which gives it the appearance of anticipating the adult modes of the later century.

There is little hint in 1760 of the outbreak of fantasy in hairdressing which was to take place before the end of the decade.

1760—1765

THE end of the Seven Years' War made social intercourse with France once more possible, and the influence of French modes was suddenly renewed. French hairdressers, milliners, and modistes arrived in London in considerable numbers and found ready patrons among the wealthy English aristocracy. Englishmen and women began to pay visits to Paris and to bring new fashions with them on their return.

Among other novelties was an adjustable farthingale. This was an arrangement of hoops, or rather of iron ribs encased in leather, and extending sideways from the waist of the wearer in such a way that they could be raised at will. In their normal position they extended horizontally outwards, the material of the dress hanging straight from them to the ground, with the result that the skirt (if so monstrous an object can be called a skirt), presented an oblong outline, broader than it was high. The ingenuity of the new arrangement lay in the fact that the main bars of the structure were hinged at the wearer's waist, so that the whole apparatus could be raised at each side like the two halves of the Tower Bridge, and so make it possible to pass through doorways and narrow lanes. A modification of this fashion persisted, in Court dress, into the nineteenth century.

Waists were very tight and long, with a pointed bodice, often of satin, and cut very low. To protect the chest from cold, a " breast-front " of lace and ribbons was worn, but even with this, women's dress, even in the daytime, presented an aspect of *décolletage* somewhat startling to modern notions. In winter small capes were worn as well as all-enveloping cloaks, and in the early seventeen-sixties small feather muffs were popular, both with men and women. For the woman the muff also served in place of the as yet uninvented handbag. When muffs grew larger people were in the habit of carrying small pet dogs in them.

1765—1770

THE second half of the seventeen-sixties was a period of tranquil prosperity for England. The Indian and Canadian conquests had swollen the Empire to proportions undreamed of in an earlier age. The English colonies in North America, although restive, had not yet broken away, and the British fleet was supreme in the waters of the world. An enormous increase in commerce resulted, affecting fashion by the importation of foreign, especially Oriental, stuffs, and also by the new wealth, not only of the London merchants, but of the lately-arisen race of those who had made licit or illicit fortunes under the none-too-strict surveillance of the East India Company.

The current variations of fashion may be briefly noted. " Hats," says a contemporary writer in *The London Chronicle*, " are now worn upon an average six inches and three-fifths broad in the brim and cocked between Quaker and Kevenhuller (*i.e.* the brims neither very loosely nor very closely attached to the crown). Some have their hats open before like a church spout . . . some wear them rather sharper like the nose of a greyhound. . . . There is a military cock and a mercantile cock, and while the beaux of St. James's wear their hats under their arms, the beaux of Moorfields all wear theirs diagonally over the left or right eye ; sailors wear their hats tucked uniformly down to the crown, and look as if they carried a triangular apple-pasty upon their heads."

The feminine coiffure, having been about the same for half a century, began to show signs of impending change. Already at the end of the seventeen-sixties woman had begun to abandon the small " head " and to pile the hair up from the forehead, in anticipation of the extravagant modes of the middle 'seventies. It was a definite breaking away from the close, simple hairdressing which had reigned supreme ever since the abandonment of the high Fontange or " commode " of lace and ribbon.

1760—1770

AS early as 1763 the Master Peruke Makers of London presented a petition to George III. in which they complained that gentlemen had begun to wear their own hair. The petition was without effect, for fashion is a heartless goddess and cares not how many honest tradesmen are ruined by her caprices. But the tendency was as yet little more than a tendency, and wigs continued to be worn by almost every man of any social pretensions for a generation longer. In 1770 there was a temporary fashion for round hats, forecasting the mode of the end of the century when the *tricorne* was definitely abandoned.

Innumerable varieties of neck-cloths were worn simultaneously, and there is little to add to what has already been said on the subject. Just as to-day one may see the " butterfly " collar, the " turn-down " collar, and the soft collar which is derived from it, wedded to bows and ties, so in the period 1760 to 1770 contemporaries were wearing lace cravats, neck-cloths fastening at the back, and the black ribbon " solitaire " fastened in front with a jewelled pin.

The three sleeves illustrated on the opposite page show varying degrees of elaboration but with an undoubted trend towards simplicity and the ultimate adoption of a purely formal turn-back of the cuff.

In 1760 powder was still worn, but women's hair was dressed rather simply, sometimes being drawn back from the face *à la Chinoise*, and surmounted by a small knot of coloured silk ribbon. Round the throat could be worn a ruche of the same material as the dress, and a fichu was draped across the shoulders not only for warmth, but as a necessary article of dress, for bodices were sometimes cut so low as to be hardly decent. Some kind of cap was almost universally worn, and could either envelop the whole head like a hood, surround the face with a fringe of lace, or rest daintily on the top of the coiffure.

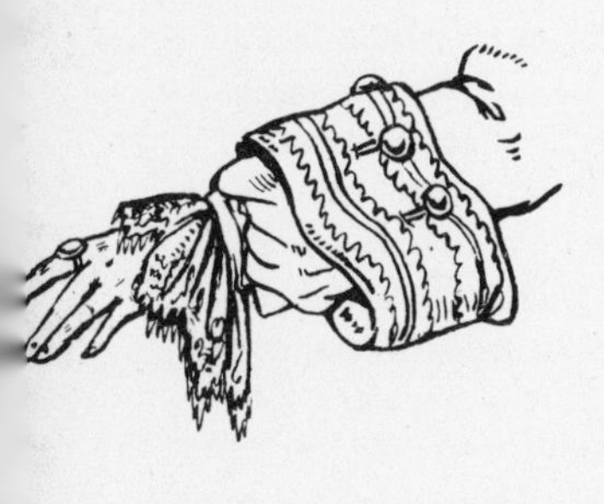
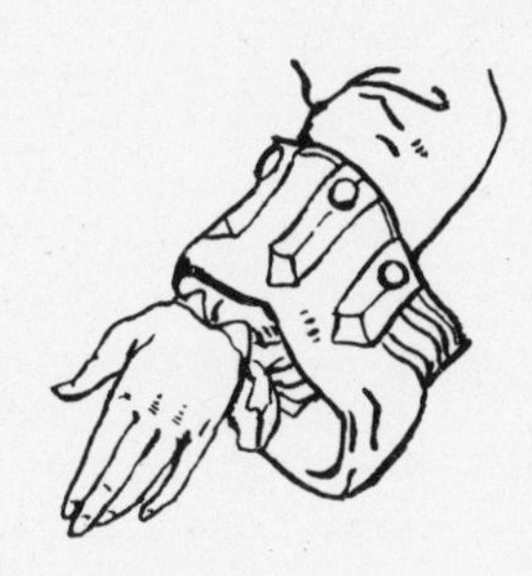

1770

THE remarkable feature of the 'seventies of the eighteenth century was the size of women's head-dresses. The change had begun in the late 'sixties, from the " snug " hairdressing of the previous decade to veritable mountains of frizz, stretched over wire frames and sometimes surmounted by fantastic structures resembling ships or windmills or gardens. As few ladies had sufficient hair of their own to comply with the new fashion, false locks were added, wool was used to fill up the interstices, and the whole was then liberally greased with pomatum and heavily dusted with white or grey powder. The dressing of such " heads " was an elaborate and costly business, so elaborate and costly that ladies of limited means had the operation performed as seldom as possible, with horribly unhygienic results.

For men, the bag-wig was very fashionable, and round the throat, the solitaire, in place of a cravat, was increasingly popular. Dandies (although the name, if not the thing itself, is an anachronism) wore flower buttonholes, often of roses, renewed every morning, like the orchid of Joseph Chamberlain in a later age. The coat-cuffs were embroidered, and the buckles of the shoe set with precious stones or paste. The colours of men's clothes were brighter than they had been earlier in the century, but simpler in cut, with shorter waistcoats and tail-coats tending somewhat to the shape of the " cut-away." Coats for formal wear were elaborately and often beautifully embroidered, with sprays of silk thread flowers on the cuffs, round the seams, and on the tails. Buttonholes became formalised, and collars were heavily decorated with needlework. Lace, however, was less in evidence as the century advanced, and as sleeves became longer and tighter there was less opportunity for its display.

1770—1775

CLOSE caps, resembling night-caps, were much worn in 1773, even in fashionable circles. Sometimes they had lace " wings " at the sides, giving a somewhat grotesque appearance to the head when seen from behind.

For a very short period men attempted to vie with women in the height of their head-dresses. The wig was built up with the aid of padding, or else rose steeply from the forehead in a kind of exaggerated *toupet*, with or without the support of a wire frame. As at the very beginning of the century when the full-bottomed wig had assumed such enormous proportions, it was now almost impossible for hats to be worn. The solution of the problem, however, was not, as it had been, to make the hat larger. On the contrary it became even smaller, and was never worn at all but merely carried in the hand and placed under the arm. Indeed, in polite society it became the masculine equivalent of the feminine fan.

This appurtenance of the toilet played a great part in eighteenth-century life. The rigid fan of the sixteenth century was an awkward engine compared with the graceful folding fan of the eighteenth. It could be carried easily, expanded quickly, and used both for cooling the face in the terribly overheated ballrooms of the period, and as an instrument of coquetry to add piquancy to smiling eyes, to conceal a blush, or to stifle a yawn. The mere fact that it could be folded within bone or ivory handles made it possible to use delicate materials such as silk or chicken-skin parchment, and to employ the best artists to paint exquisite little scenes thereon. Sometimes the fan, like the snuff-box, had a proper and a " gallant " side, either of which could be turned outwards at the will of the user. Some of the eighteenth-century fans which have come down to us are miracles of a delicate artistry which has never been surpassed.

1775—1780

THE head-dress of women reached its most fantastic height in the middle 'seventies; indeed, it almost seems as if the growing tendency for men to wear their own hair, or at least to combine more and more of their own hair with a diminishing wig, spurred the perruquiers on to invent even more elaborate head-dresses for women in order to keep themselves in employment. The dressing of a head for a fashionable function occupied three or four hours. With head-dresses of such enormous size it was essential for ladies to have hats to match, although sometimes a comparatively small hat was worn pinned firmly on top of the coiffure. Sometimes the hat was a part of the hairdressing, or, rather, the latter was so elaborate as to render a hat superfluous.

Bonnets of satin, taffeta, or linen were worn by women of all classes *en négligé*, *i.e.* on any occasion when full dress was not required, such as going to church or for a morning walk.

Long walking-sticks with gold or silver knobs were carried both by men and women, and the practice of wearing swords fell more and more into disuse, except among military men.

About the year 1778 a fashion arose of trimming the diagonal front edges of the overskirt with a frill of the same material as the flounces of the sleeves. The overskirt was sometimes puffed out with a stuffing of loosely crumpled paper which made a strange rustling noise when the wearer moved. The underskirt was richly ornamented either with horizontal gathers of its own material or with strips of lace, ribbon, or fur. The two skirts were frequently of contrasting colours or of lighter and deeper shades of the same colour. The skirt with *paniers*, before its final disappearance, was worn short, showing the shoes and the ankles, and, as always, a shorter skirt led to increased care for the neatness of shoes and stockings.

1770—1780

FROM the end of the seventeenth-seventies there is, quite suddenly, an enormous increase in the number of documents which may be consulted by the student of fashion. In a word, the fashion plate springs into being, and it is interesting to note that some of the earliest fashion plates were not concerned with the whole costume but with the method of dressing the hair. The fantastic hairdressing fashions of the decade made ladies all the more eager to be aware of the latest mode, and the engravers and publishers were not long in satisfying their curiosity.

A publication with the interesting title of *Souvenir à l'Anglaise et Recueil de Coëffures* appeared in Paris in 1778, and there was soon a rage for such aids to modernity on both sides of the Channel. The fashion paper was fairly launched and no doubt contributed largely to a more rapid changing of modes than had been customary or, indeed, possible earlier in the century. It is probable that the vogue for caricatures may have contributed to the same effect, for by exaggerating each fashion in turn and so tending to make it ridiculous, the growth of new fashions was stimulated. In England, however, the great growth of fashion plates belongs rather to the turn of the century than to the decade now under discussion.

Masculine hairdressing became neater and closer to the head, the three-cornered hat being very small and worn far forward, so that the brim came just above the eyes. Sleeves were sometimes extremely narrow, with a simple edge of lace protruding from the cuff. The formalised buttons and buttonholes, which had once had the genuine function of keeping the turned-back cuff in place, remained on the sleeve as decoration, just as they have remained to this day, sometimes as many as four, sometimes one, but never entirely absent. The *vestigial* element in dress is always large and is a proof of the extraordinary conservatism of fashion beneath all its apparent change.

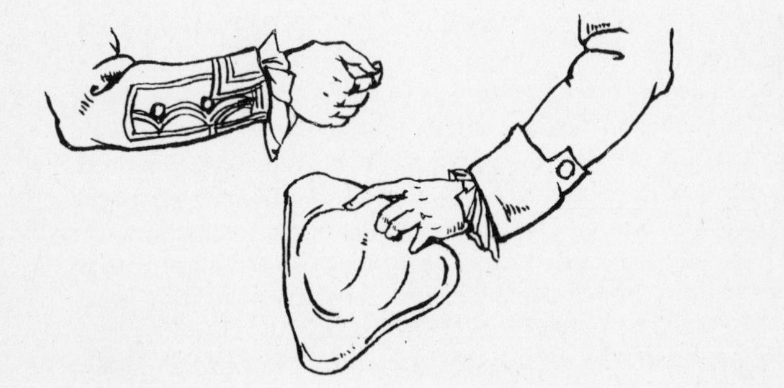

1780

BY the year 1780 the revived farthingale or hoop may be said to have disappeared, its place being taken by small pads or cushions fastened to the hips, and then by a single pad at the back. In fact, the eighteenth-century equivalent of the crinoline was followed by the eighteenth-century equivalent of the bustle, although neither of the names had as yet been invented. The recurrence of fashion is an attractive theory, but such recurrence obeys some peculiar rhythm of its own, so that prophecy becomes difficult if not impossible. There is, none the less, a certain parallelism between the course of fashion in the eighteenth and in the nineteenth centuries, even in small and seemingly unimportant details.

The fashion of embroidering men's coats all over their surface had now been abandoned. Even waistcoats were not so highly ornamented as they had been, the embroidery being now generally confined to the skirts, the pockets, and the buttonholes.

There was a reaction against high heels and a forecasting of the almost completely heelless shoes of the early nineteenth century. Improvements in the craft of shoemaking made all shoes much more comfortable, so that the use of house-slippers was abandoned. The long tongue of the upper disappeared almost completely.

For women, the large horizontal hat, usually worn at an engaging angle and adorned with ribbons or feathers, began to be fashionable in 1780, or soon afterwards. The material of these hats was straw or silk or some light foundation, and it was securely fastened to the coiffure with pins to prevent it from falling off. Even so it must have been no light task to manage the head-dress of the period in a high wind. Men were beginning to grow tired of the universal *tricorne* and to cock their hats in a different way—straight up and down at the front and back, so that the two edges lay together. The hat thus treated was the ancestor of all the " Napoleonic " hats and of the cocked hats of modern admirals and generals.

1780—1785

ABOUT the year 1780 there was a wave of simplicity, not the real simplicity of the time of the Revolution, but a pseudo-pastoralism derived from the example of Marie Antoinette at the Trianon. There the ladies of the Court played at being shepherdesses and dressed their hair in "milkmaid" or "peasant" fashion, but dresses were no less costly for being pastoral or pseudo-pastoral. The influence of the country was more effective in England, where there was a real enthusiasm for rural life and where men, at least, wore clothes suitable for hard weather and boots adapted to the muddiness of the roads. Some women, finding a semi-masculine riding-dress becoming, adopted it for morning wear whether they intended to ride or not. The bodice was made in imitation of a man's coat and waistcoat with overlapping revers, and the skirt was full, but simple and without trimming. On ordinary dresses trimmings were abandoned in favour of ruches of muslin or lace, arranged in flounces and sewn to the edge of the dress. Gowns were worn rather long, and the white stockings were invisible. About the year 1783 there was a rage for decorating dresses with straw, even men's waistcoats being ribbed with it, and straw coats, called *paillasses*, were worn by women.

About 1780 hats began to be perched on the top of the high coiffures, with the result that the head-dress itself grew smaller to accommodate them. Hair was crimped and arranged in "hedgehog" fashion, puffed out from the face, and hats had to be very large in order to cover it without spoiling the effect. Some of the mob-caps of the period were almost as large as hoods and, indeed, resembled them very closely. On more formal hats there was a rage for ostrich feathers, a fashion immortalised by Gainsborough in his portrait of the Duchess of Devonshire.

1785—1790

TOWARDS the end of the 'eighties it became the fashion for women to wear a separate jacket-like garment called a *caraco*. This was close-fitting and made in a masculine style. Beneath it a tight-fitting dress was worn, bodice and skirt of the same material, the skirt contrasting with the *caraco*, which came more than ever to resemble a man's dress-coat. Sometimes the under-dress was without a bodice, a light corset being worn in its place, concealed by a kind of front or stomacher, made to resemble a man's waistcoat. This very masculine attire was sometimes worn with a large apron with pockets.

In winter *mantelets* were worn. These were short capes of silk occasionally edged with fur. When fitted with wide, half-length sleeves, the winter garment was called a *pelisse*.

From 1786 there was a fashion for beaver hats similar to those worn by men, but more richly trimmed.

The three-cornered hat may be said to have disappeared after the French Revolution. Shoe-buckles also fell out of fashion, being replaced by shoe-strings, although the growing use of boots rendered both unnecessary.

The heels of women's shoes were lower than they had been throughout the century, and the upper was more open, ending a couple of inches behind the toes. Shoes were more comfortably made, with the result that walking became more fashionable.

Swords, which had been worn throughout the century, disappeared about 1786, except with Court dress. About the same period, the wide skirts of men's coats gave place to long tails. Coats were double-breasted and very short in front, so as to reveal the waistcoat. In 1790 there was a temporary fashion for black coats, but the breeches and waistcoats remained brilliant in colour. Waistcoats and stockings were ornamented with vertical or horizontal stripes.

1780—1790

THE collars of men's coats, non-existent in the earlier part of the century, could be worn turned over in the modern fashion or else standing rigidly round the neck. The space between the neck and the collar was filled with a scarf wound several times round—the ancestor of the modern neck-tie. This neck-scarf was often of muslin, as its predecessor had been of cambric. Sleeves became still narrower and very long, so that little of the fine frills at the end of the shirt sleeve could be seen.

One of the fashionable methods of dressing the hair was to have two or three horizontal curls at the side and a little formal queue at the back. This mode has persisted, in a smaller, somewhat stylised form, in the barristers' wig of to-day, so that while the judge on the bench wears a wig dating in shape from the beginning of the eighteenth century, the wigs of counsel date from about 1780. State coachmen's wigs, worn by the coachmen of the nobility until the beginning of the twentieth century, date from the same period as those of barristers.

The typical head-dress of the seventeen-eighties for women tended to width, just as that of the 'seventies had tended to height. The effect was somewhat suggestive of the loose hair of a cavalier during the reign of Charles I. Over the hair large mob-caps could be worn, or else a broad-brimmed straw hat very simply trimmed. The general appearance could be charming. The hair, except on formal occasions, was worn without powder, but curling was essential if only to expand the hair to the required size. A kind of hood made of crape was very fashionable, and as the hair completely filled it, it was impossible to tell whether it was a hood or a cap. In winter hoods were edged with fur. Caps persisted for many years, and certain combinations of black and white lace remained as an old lady's head-dress in remote places for nearly a century.

1790

IN masculine attire the beginning of the seventeen-nineties marked the victory of English modes over French ones, and the beginning of a dominance which they have maintained ever since. The " European dress " established at the beginning of the century by the prestige of the French Court now gave place to a coat recognisably similar to that worn to-day in evening-dress.

The cut of the masculine coat had been fixed for so long that it must have seemed difficult, if not impossible, to change it. Ever since the evolution of coat and waistcoat at the end of the seventeenth century, the relationship of these two articles of attire had been constant. Now some genius adapted the double-breasted coat from the English riding-coat with its two rows of buttons, and two far-reaching consequences immediately followed, both caused by the necessity of keeping a double-breasted coat fastened if it is to preserve its fit. Had the coat been as long in front as formerly the wearer would have been considerably hampered in his movements, and the waistcoat—which had always provided an opportunity for the display of the wearer's taste—would have been totally concealed. Thus tailors began to experiment by cutting the front of the coat away. The period also witnessed an orgy of " revers," even waistcoats being provided with them, often of a colour contrasting with those of the coat.

As the waistcoat pockets were no longer easily accessible, it became the fashion to wear the watch in a front pocket of the breeches. Sometimes both front pockets carried a watch, with seals dangling down outside. The remote successors of these dangling seals were worn into the twentieth century, and may still occasionally be seen, but as the trousers have no front pockets, the " fob " is fastened to the braces.

1790—1795

DURING the early days of the Revolution in France, and most of all during "the Terror," it became positively dangerous to be seen in the streets of Paris in rich clothes. Not only was the cut plainer, but the materials also. Silks and satins disappeared, their place being taken by cotton, Indian print, and lawn. In England, there was less reason for change, not only because of the stability of the Government, but because the English gentleman with his country habits wore, by preference, clothes much less gaudy than those of his French counterpart. From one point of view, the Revolution was a victory for English fashions, even in France. The top-boots, the unembroidered coats, the stout breeches made for much hard wear in the saddle, passed from the country into the town, and men entered drawing-rooms in costumes more suited to the hunting-field. But Englishmen never adopted the extremely high and voluminous neck-clothes which in France actually rose to cover the chin and sometimes the mouth. A short bamboo cane or riding-whip replaced the long walking-stick of a few years before.

In women's costume, England almost entirely escaped the worst extravagances of the French *merveilleuses*, who went about the streets of Paris in a costume supposed to be Greek, consisting of one semi-transparent chemise-like dress with pink skin-tights worn underneath. The girdle was placed immediately under the breasts, and this fashion reached England towards the end of the century, when very high waists came into fashion. The rage for tall feathers also came from France—a little late, for they had been introduced by Marie Antoinette. It is curious to reflect that the custom of wearing two feathers upright in the hair, which began in this period, has lasted, in Court dress, until our own time.

1795—1800

In the middle 'nineties, or, in extremely fashionable circles, just before, the short waist became the rage. The waist, in fact, slipped up to immediately below the breasts and remained there for about twenty years. The materials used for dresses were very thin, but unlike those employed in the days of *paniers*, they were neither used in great quantities nor elaborately patterned. Simplicity was pushed to the verge of indecency, although the transparent dresses worn in France were never popular in England. We have seen that at the beginning of the century English manufacturers were complaining of the importation of calicoes from India; now, owing chiefly to the invention by Arkwright of the spinning frame, the position was reversed, and the East India Company was driven to complain of the harm done to its import trade by the successful manufacture of British cottons and muslins.

The scantiness of dresses led to the popularity of large fur muffs and to the introduction of wraps, cashmere shawls, or sometimes mere handkerchiefs disposed like a fichu to protect the throat. A short, close-fitting coat with long sleeves, called the spencer, appeared about 1797.

In thin and unvoluminous dresses with no under-petticoats, women, at the end of the eighteenth century, found themselves confronted by a new problem—that of pockets. Their absence led to the invention of the reticule or handbag. It was much laughed at, but has survived several periods of eclipse, to become, in our own day, the most necessary accessory of female costume.

High-heeled shoes began to be discarded in favour of coloured slippers, made of satin for evening wear and of Morocco leather for day-time. They were extremely flimsy, for only eccentric young women, like Wordsworth's "dear child of Nature," went for long walks in the country.

1790—1800

IN 1795 Pitt imposed a tax on hair-powder, and so almost extinguished a fashion which was already on the wane, although true-blue Tories still continued to wear both wigs and hair-powder as a patriotic gesture, and to distinguish them from those who sympathised with the French Revolution. Political opinions sometimes decided the colour of a man's clothes. The Tory supporters of Pitt wore scarlet waistcoats, while the Whigs who supported Fox wore yellow. The partisans of Fox had also the very odd habit of carrying large red-fox muffs.

Sleeves became simpler than ever, the turned-back cuff being altogether abandoned, or else symbolised rather than imitated by a band of braid. The number of buttons worn on sleeves was also noticeably reduced.

About the year 1795 caps were discarded in fashionable circles in favour of bandeaux or fillets in supposed imitation of classical models. These fillets were made of muslin or of strips of coloured embroidery. Very few English women in these years of hostility to France followed the French fashion of having their hair cut short at the back and hanging in dishevelled locks over the face, *à la Titus*. A few may be noticed, however, particularly in the charming stipple engravings of Adam Buck.

From 1794 to 1797 there was a fashion for enormous ostrich plumes in the hair, sometimes two or three of different colours being worn together. The plainness of the dress of the period seemed to demand the wearing of jewellery, but as diamonds and other precious stones were temporarily out of fashion, semi-precious stones and corals were fashioned into cameos in imitation of the antique. Everything, in fact, was antique or pseudo-antique, and the century which began with the stiff splendour of the *Grand Siècle* ends in an orgy of the neo-classical.

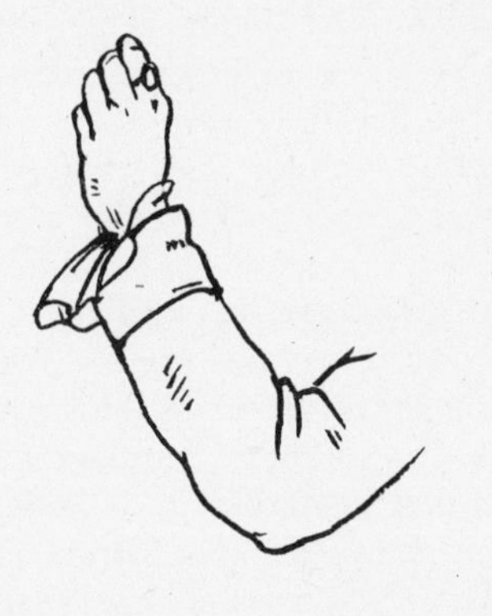
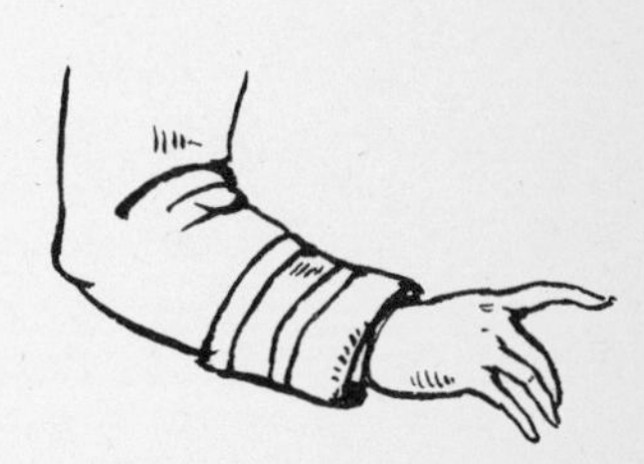

English Costume of the Nineteenth Century

FOREWORD

It was in the Nineteenth Century that the Modern World took shape, and it would be strange indeed if the political and economic revolutions which determined the history of Europe during that hundred years should have found no reflection in the evolution of our clothes. In their hatred of the embroidered garments of the nobility, the men and women of 1789 turned, on the one hand, to English country fashions, and, on the other, to what they imagined was the clothing of the Ancient Greeks. The result was that top-boots for men and a single, flimsy, chemise-like garb for women became the accepted wear. Men abandoned knee-breeches, long flapped surcoats and wigs; women gave up loops, brocade and the use of powder on the hair. But the greatest revolution of all was that henceforth the classes could no longer be distinguished by striking differences of dress. Yet changes in fashion, especially for women, happened all the more frequently, for only by adopting the very latest novelty could the woman of wealth distinguish herself from her sisters. For a whole century the accepted forms of male and female costume had remained fundamentally the same. Once the tradition was broken, anything might have happened. What actually did happen, and how we arrived by easy stages at something approaching the dress of to-day, it is the purpose of the following pages to show.

J. L.

1836

1800

IN the time of the French Directory, during the first flush of freedom from the old eighteenth-century modes, women's dress had pushed daring to the point of indecency, and men's, with its immense tails and prodigious neckcloth, had been more fantastic than the style it had superseded. But by 1800 sobriety had won its victory. Feminine dress was still in one piece, divided into skirt and bodice by a cord or ribbon tied immediately under the breasts. A short jacket was sometimes added as a protection against the cold—a protection much needed, as the garments of the day were scantier even than those of modern times.

The materials used were excessively light muslin, batiste, lawn—and the caricaturists made merry over the disasters of revelation consequent upon the slightest sudden shower. Gérard's painting of Psyche set a fashion for white dresses which was very generally followed. The wild hair of 1794 had been drawn closer to the head, but it was still short both for men and women. Men's coats had assumed the cut-away shape which persists to-day in formal evening and morning dress. Their neckcloths had shrunk to moderate proportions and the beginnings of the modern bow-tie were apparent. Breeches had not yet been entirely abandoned, but were already on their last legs. The three-cornered hat with plumes had disappeared, and the ancestor of the silk-hat was already taking shape.

1800—1805

SOON after the beginning of the century, women began to be bored with the single garment, and to wear over it a second, cut open in front or short in the form of a tunic. The romantic elements of the late eighteenth century began to break through the pseudo-classical crust, and dressmakers began to puff the sleeves in the manner of the Tudor period and to encircle the neck with the beginnings of a high lace frill. Already in 1801, ruffs made of Brabant lace, and called "Betsies," after Queen Elizabeth, had made their appearance, and although the high waist continued, revolutionary simplicity was gone for ever. The poke-bonnet, which was afterwards to attain to such formidable dimensions, had been known as early as 1797, and by 1805 had begun to be common.

Men's hats, in that warlike age, were sometimes cocked in the military or naval fashion, but the high-crowned beaver was already winning its way to universal acceptance. In masculine clothes the ascendancy of Brummel was establishing the reputation of English tailors for fineness of cut which has persisted until to-day. An ideal of cleanliness was adopted both of the clothes and of the person, which is one of the debts which the modern world owes to the early nineteenth-century dandy.

1805—1810

AFTER 1805 the new style may be said to have become established. The dress fitted closely, but no longer trailed on the ground as before. The train of the early years of the century was abolished, and the skirt began to be worn shorter. By 1808, in some garments at least, the feet were free, and two years later ankles were visible. The shawl had made its first appearance in England as long ago as 1786, but it became the rage during the first ten years of the new century. The passion for " draperies " encouraged the use of shawls, and cashmere became extremely fashionable. Even the introduction of fur cloaks from Vienna about 1808 failed to displace the shawl, and it continued to be worn until quite late in the century. Nothing in women's dress, however, was of such importance as what was happening to men's—the triumph of trousers. Originally the costume of the English sailor or the French *sans-culotte*, they gradually made their way into the most fashionable society. Soon only elderly men were to be seen wearing breeches, and after Waterloo they may be said to have disappeared from ordinary attire.

1800—1810

THE first ten years of the century witnessed, as we have seen, the beginning of the poke-bonnet, and the development of men's linen and neckcloths along the lines they have followed ever since. The frilled shirt, allowed to project through a very low-cut waistcoat, became the ancestor of the modern evening-dress shirt, and it is curious to note that the soft shirt with many pleats, which made its appearance after the European War, was in reality less of a novelty than a revival.

Hair, which about 1798 had begun to be cut quite short, was, in the early years of the new century, brushed forward over the eyes. By 1809 it was the fashion to curl it, and shortly afterwards was adopted the plain short cut which has existed, with minor modifications, ever since. Women's hair began to be worn longer.

1810

THE general dress of the day was plainer, both for men and women, than it had been for centuries, but ceremonial dress was still worn at the English Court, and Napoleon re-introduced it into his own. Indeed, in spite of the war against England, the winter of 1809–10, just before Napoleon's second marriage, was the most brilliant and extravagant season of any that had been seen since the fall of the *ancien régime*. Men's fashions had firmly adopted the English mode, but women's continued to be inspired by Paris. The turban, which is said to have been inspired by the campaigns in Egypt, had become a recognised item of feminine attire. Stays came in during the winter of 1809 and persisted for a century.

1810-1815

EVEN in winter, morning dresses continued to be made of muslin, although bombazine (then considered a very elegant material) was also worn. Dinner dresses were made of velvet and satin. Velvet frocks trimmed with swansdown were popular about 1812. Collars, for day wear, became noticeably higher, and short sleeves disappeared. In the evening, gowns were cut square over the bosom and very low. Shoulder straps entirely disappeared. Dresses were trimmed with frills or rolls of the same material, and it was not until 1812 that different coloured trimmings began to be used. The article of attire most characteristic of the period was the pelisse, a kind of over-dress, buttoning down the front, and sometimes made fairly short in order to show nine or ten inches of a white muslin dress underneath. In very severe weather a "pilgrim's cloak" was thrown over the pelisse. Furs also were worn in cold weather, and ankle-boots for women made their appearance. They were almost heelless, but still pointed, and sometimes laced behind. Slippers had slashings of contrasting colours. Gold ornaments began to replace the coloured stones which had previously been popular.

In men's dress, trousers are seen to have won their triumph, and the astonishing reign of the tall hat has been successfully inaugurated. Some older features of dress, however, still persisted, notably the coat with many overlapping capes, which survived among coachmen even later. Waistcoats once more came down to the hips.

1815-1820

THE beginning of the long peace marked a considerable change in the general shape of women's dresses. The waist became even shorter than it had been before, and the skirt descended from it in straight lines to just above the ankles. The bottom of the skirt, however, was very much wider and much more decorated, generally with somewhat stiff *rouleaux* of material—a kind of incipient (and external) crinoline. The use of transparent materials worn over opaque ones began to be appreciated, and it became fashionable to wear a frock of pink crape over a slip of white satin, or a dress of net (the name " patent net " shows how recently it had been invented) over a slip of coloured satin or sarsnet. Sleeves became very elaborate, and the exaggeration of the shoulders foreshadowed the fashions of the 'thirties. Puckered muslin was used to give to sleeves the puffed appearance of the time of Henry VIII, and the Tudor ruff round the neck emphasized the period from which dressmakers were drawing their inspiration. The influence of Scott was also to be seen in the fashion for plaid scarves and sashes, which were very popular about 1817.

Men's fashions exhibited no change worth recording.

1810-1820

THE military enthusiasms of the time are seen in the adoption for women's dress of details from soldiers' uniforms. Even the forms of headgear were copied, and froggings and epaulettes gave an added touch of patriotic fantasy. The so-called Wellington hat, the Wellington bonnet, and even the Wellington jacket (made of twilled sarsnet and worn for dinner parties) were extremely popular. There was also a Wellington mantle, like a small Spanish cloak, and it is sad to think that the name of the great soldier, having rested lightly for a moment on so many articles of attire, should, in the end, have clung only to boots.

What was known as the plain cottage bonnet became somewhat more elaborate, being cut out in front so as to display a lace cap underneath. Hats became higher and were decorated with flowers, feathers, or bands of plaited "grogram" or puffed gauze. At this period, and much later, hats were worn in the evening with everything but full dress, for which flowers or feathers were substituted.

Ostrich plumes became fashionable, and, worn upright in the hair, they have persisted for court dress until to-day.

Men's collars continued to be high, and the neck-cloth was still voluminous.

1820

ALTHOUGH white was still fashionable, coloured dresses were sometimes worn, and, as a somewhat daring innovation, a coloured bodice with a white skirt. The waistband, which was occasionally coloured even when the dress was white, sank to its normal position immediately above the hips. Sleeves continued to be puffed and slashed in a pseudo-Elizabethan style. The hat was large, and plumes, sometimes of various colours, were much worn.

Drawers, long, tight-fitting, and trimmed with lace, began to be worn by women, although they were not universal until the 'thirties, or later. Little girls also wore them long, so that they protruded several inches below the skirts, and, had they not been so elaborate, would have looked like trousers. Sometimes these " pantalettes " were false, being merely attached by tapes above the knee.

Trousers for men were by this time almost universal, their supremacy never to be disputed until the coming of knickerbockers at the very end of the century. The tall hat was broad-brimmed, with the crown wider at the top than at the bottom. The collar of the shirt rose almost to the sides of the mouth, and the front of the shirt was frilled and allowed to protrude through the waistcoat.

1820-1825

LITTLE change was seen in women's dress during the early 'twenties. The waist remained high and bodices, which were very short, had a *bouffant* drapery over the bust, sometimes made of silk netting, to give (in the words of a contemporary chronicle) a fullness where nature had been less prodigal. Ball dresses were short, and the padded *rouleau* at the bottom gave them that weighted appearance so typical of the period. They were made of striped crape, flock gauze, rainbow gauze, plain *barège*, silk or tulle. Colours were tender rather than violent, the favourites being lavender grey, pale yellow, mignonette-green, and rose. Scarlet ball dresses were, however, not unknown. Hats were large and elaborate, being lined with velvet and trimmed with large plumes. There was a passion for feathers, and they were considered essential even on "satin bonnets for the morning lounge." Trimmings were sometimes of polished steel. Turbans of figured gauze were the favourite head-dresses of married ladies of middle age. For evening wear they were adorned with a few pearls or, in mourning, with a bandeau of jet or bugles, and a plume of feathers. Young ladies wore wreaths of flowers made of crape.

For men, the fit of clothes became even more important than it had previously been. The tails of a dress-coat were now cut out separately and sewn onto the body of the coat, so that the latter followed the figure more closely. Hips and chest were exaggerated by padding. Trousers either ended well above the ankles or were cut long enough to be strapped under the boots.

1825-1830

ALREADY, by 1827, the sleeves of gowns had begun to assume the swollen appearance so typical of the next decade. In ball dresses they looked like enormous epaulettes, which indeed was the name given to them. Skirts were growing wider, and the turned-down white collars larger, the Vandyke succeeding the Elizabethan. Hats were rounder and perched more on the top of the head. They were sometimes made of fine straw and worn over a small lace cap. Very long ribbons of the same colours as the trimming of the hat floated over the shoulders.

Chintzes came into favour for morning dresses, and for home costume during the day. Cambric skirts were bordered with shawl material, and a reticule of the same stuff was carried in the hand.

The corsage was longer in the waist than it had been, and the pleats of the skirt were gathered into the band, giving an equal fullness all round. This was known as the Dutch fashion, and did not last very long. Waists were very tight. Shawls of red cashmere were much worn as an outdoor covering.

1820-1830

TO the modern eye there is something very astonishing in the apparent unwillingness of women of the 'twenties ever to have their heads completely uncovered. The minimum for morning wear was an elaborate lace cap, and for evening, a towering wreath or some large ornament of metal. Very big hats with plumes were worn for dinner parties, and even at the opera—it is to be hoped, only by those who sat in boxes. Even so, a hat as broad as the lady's shoulders adorned with half-a-dozen immense ostrich feathers cannot have added much to the enjoyment of the attendant gallant.

Hair was sometimes parted on the forehead *à la Madonna*, with ringlets over each temple descending nearly as low as the tip of the ear. Sprigs of flowers were scattered among the bows in the hair, such bows being of coloured gauze ribbon striped with silver. Very high ornamental tortoiseshell combs were not unknown towards the end of the decade. They sustained two large curls, known as the Apollo's knot. Ball dresses were cut fairly low in a boat shape, and were very elaborately trimmed at the edge of the corsage.

1830

THE distinguishing feature of women's dress in the 'thirties was its enormous breadth caused by the width of the skirt and the extreme fullness of the sleeves. Skirts were short, and this exaggerated the squat impression of the whole costume. The sleeves were so voluminous, even in evening-dress, that they had to be kept extended by wicker frames or even by small feather cushions.

Hair-dressing was very elaborate, the hair being built up from the head and crowned with flowers, feathers, or jewelled combs. During the mourning for George IV, black and white crape flowers were used to decorate the hair in full dress.

Leghorn, rice straw, and *gros de Naples* were the materials most in favour for promenade hats, the brims of which were very wide, and cut so as to conceal as little of the face as possible. They were trimmed with dahlias, anemones, and field-flowers, sometimes mingled with ears of corn.

Full dress tended to be fairly simple, muslin being most usual; and, when mourning was over, this was generally white. If coloured, dresses were of one colour only, the favourites being rose, blue, or lilac.

1830-1835

IN the early 'thirties corsages were tight at the waist and long, the heart-shaped bodice being the most popular. Velvet was very much worn, even in combination with silk. Crape, and a material called "blond," were also used, and it was possible to have a dress *à la Taglioni* of tulle worked in lamy. Printed satins were much in use for scarfs and shawls. Poplin dresses were trimmed with satin bows. Quite young women at balls or parties wore brocaded gauze dresses of pink or white, or white organdie dresses, with a rose in the hair and a rose at the girdle. Fashionable colours of the early 'thirties were pink, blue, "grenat," *violet de Parme*, and lapis-lazuli; but yellow was a favourite colour for ball dresses.

Shoes were flat-heeled and square-toed, and for evening wear were generally of black satin. Silk stockings were very fine and transparent, but it was the custom to wear another pair underneath, of flesh-coloured cashmere.

The so-called Grecian coiffure was very fashionable, but hair was also worn in plain bands or with ringlets wide apart on the temples and descending low on the cheeks.

1835-1840

THE place of the fichu was taken by various kinds of collar, generally worn low and turned back. Collars could be made of plain velvet or of watered silk embroidered in colour. Tight sleeves or sleeves enlarging just above the elbow (known as sleeves *à la jardinière*) took the place of the exaggerated sleeves of the early part of the decade. Skirts became considerably longer, and, as their weight was becoming oppressive, Paris dressmakers, in 1839, introduced a modified form of hoop which could be added to or disengaged from the corset at pleasure. However, the *crino zephir* (or horse-hair tissue under petticoats) was still worn.

Shawls were worn even in summer, when they were made of muslin, lace, or net. Plain cashmere shawls with deep fringes were also fashionable.

Children's dresses were mostly made of muslin or cambric with lace insertion.

There was considerable elaboration of such details of the toilette as handkerchiefs. These were sometimes embroidered in red, blue, or brown, with the name of the owner in Gothic characters, surmounted by her coat-of-arms. Black silk mittens were extremely common.

1830-1840

DURING the early 'thirties curls were much worn, and sometimes these were supported by wire frames and ornamental combs.

Towards the end of the decade the coiffure became very much lower, and many women, especially among the young, wore twists of hair falling on the neck, fastened with Italian pins. Long ringlets made their appearance, and sometimes the hair falling on the cheek was twisted spirally and the ends placed behind the ears.

The poke-bonnet was almost universal, but an attempt was made to raise it from the face by pulling down the brim at the sides. Then the crown was lowered, and at the end of the decade the whole hat was much smaller, although the peak was still fairly high. Straw hats became very general towards 1840. They were trimmed with crape or gauze of the same colour as the hat, or with field-flowers placed very far back on the brim. About 1839 an extraordinary substitute for the cap was introduced. This was the "arcade," which consisted of three or four wires in the form of a frame round which were twined rose-buds mixed with lace and ribbon.

1840

IF women have never dressed so scantily as they did about 1800, they have probably never been so warmly clad as in the 'forties. Five or six petticoats, with much solid padding, were quite normal, and worn as they were beneath long, full skirts, were of great advantage to the unshapely woman, as they concealed her natural deficiencies almost completely. But the weight of so many garments must have been intolerable, and the crinoline, when perfected, was a genuine reform. Shawls were still fashionable, and the poke bonnet had begun to assume its most characteristic shape.

Men's clothes had not yet abandoned all colour in deference to the growing fashion for black. The form of the frock-coat gave an almost feminine appearance to the male figure. Dress-coats also were extremely waisted. Tall hats were very high, and more shiny than they had been previously. Waistcoats were still elaborate and trousers very tight.

Riding became fashionable among both sexes, and the riding-habits of the period, with tight bodices (which were later slightly modified) and long, voluminous skirts, can be well studied in early paintings of Queen Victoria.

1840-1845

MANTELETS, or scarf-mantelets, became almost universal. They were made of tarlatan and tulle, and were worn over " chameleon " silk dresses. Silk mantelets were trimmed with ruches of lace, guipure, or shaded ribbon of a contrasting colour.

The laced corsage was sometimes adopted for the opportunity it offered of showing the chemisette, which was either embroidered or composed of insertions of lace. Ribbons were extensively used for the decoration of the upper part of the dress. Negligés are the natural result of tight lacing, although some of the so-called negligés of the 'forties would seem stiff enough to a generation accustomed to lounge in pyjamas. Men also had their lounging clothes or smoking suits, generally of a pseudo-Turkish appearance.

Hats were shorter at the ears and more forward in front than they had previously been. Sometimes they were composed of puffings of tulle ornamented with shaded feathers.

Ball dresses had several skirts and were usually ornamented with flowers.

1845-1850

CORSAGES continued to be tight, and were made either of plain silk or of puckered taffeta. " Volans," or flounces, almost superseded all other trimmings for dresses, sometimes as many as eight being adopted, the highest reaching to within a few inches of the waist. They could be made of fringe or of puckered lace. Skirts without " volans " sometimes had a kind of stylised apron. Dresses of light materials such as *barège*, silk, muslin, or coloured tarlatan had the sleeves puckered at the wristband. Large shawls of black or white lace, or of cashmere, alternated with mantelets or *visites*—a *visite* being a kind of three-quarter-length coat with sleeves made of embroidered muslin or some similar material. Towards the end of the decade, and for cold weather, a short coat called a " Casaweck " made its appearance, made of wadded satin or velvet. Alternatives were Castilian or Andalusian cloaks made of satin, or velvet Hungarian cloaks lined with ermine, minever, or chinchilla.

Small girls' dresses were mostly made with double skirts and with fan-shaped corsages cut straight on the chest and shoulders. The bonnet for out-of-doors was very similar to that worn by their elders.

1840-1850

ALTHOUGH ball dresses were very low, and neck and shoulders bare, there was a surprising absence of neck-jewellery, a simple brooch in the front of the corsage being considered sufficient. Indeed, an attempt seems to have been made, in making the neck and shoulders the only unadorned portion of an elaborate toilette, to draw particular attention to them, and it is certainly true that in the evening dresses of the period the appearance given to the female form of emerging from complicated wrappings could be used by a clever dressmaker with most seductive effect.

Hats were composed of tulle, straw, gauze, and flowers. Open straw hats were fashionable for warm weather, and about 1846 there was a return to the eighteenth-century mode, with a hat *à la Clarissa Harlowe*, much worn at watering-places or in the country.

The beginning of the decade witnessed a great variety of male neck-wear. Some cravats were worn, as well as neck-cloths tied in a bow in front. Cravats gradually disappeared, however, and narrow ties, over which the shirt collar could be folded, were adopted by the younger men. The "dicky," or separate shirt-front, was no longer worn, being replaced by a shirt with an inset breast of finer linen. Side-whiskers, worn with a moustache and small "Imperial," were not uncommon, although they had not yet attained the extravagant dimensions of a few years later.

1850

A GENERAL levelling of the classes took place, caused partly by the new passion for travel introduced by the extension of railways ; but the novel social conditions, if they tended to make rank less important, made wealth more so, and, therefore, gave added impetus to the competition of elegance.

The main features of women's dress may be briefly summarised. Skirts were very full and often heavily flounced. The corsage was sometimes open to the waist, so as to allow the white under-garment to be seen, the two edges of the corset being kept together by ribbons or narrow strips of cloth attached by buttons. Fairly wide sleeves ending halfway down the forearm, with a sleeve of softer material appearing beneath and gathered in at the wrist, are very typical of the period. When a series of false sleeves of different lengths were worn they were called Pagodas, and were frequently white. Small over-jackets or "cannezouts" of white embroidered muslin, bordered with English lace, were much seen about 1850. The poke-bonnet was smaller than before and the top line of the head almost horizontal. Very few changes are to be noted in male dress.

1850-1855

THE dominating influence in European fashion was, since her marriage in November 1853, the Empress Eugénie. Perhaps her Spanish taste had something to do with the growing rage for violent colour, but for evening wear she added her own influence to the prevailing fashion for white. The materials used were embroidered muslin and tulle, and the panniers of dresses were enriched with ribbons of white taffeta placed at the edge to give the effect of lace. Morning dresses were of thicker stuff, such as worsted poplin. With summer costumes mantillas were worn (another sign of Spanish influence), as well as shawls of muslin or white tarlatan. For winter there was great variety of cloaks, the colours of which were dark: red, brown, and drab. Velvet was used as a trimming for everything—hats, cloaks, and dresses. Sometimes velvet was embroidered with beads, particularly coral, and sometimes it was cut to represent pansies or daisies.

Hats were of Italian straw with flowers within and without, and were furnished with a single broad ribbon of taffeta tied beneath the chin in a simple bow. Sometimes they were made of velvet and crape combined, or of velvet and silk, or of velvet and lace. Velvet, always velvet!

1855-1860

FASHION in the late 'fifties was singularly stable, and the only "decided novelty" which a contemporary record can discover is a slight increase in the size of bonnets. It was felt that the diminutive bonnet, hanging on the back of the head, was out of proportion to the mass of silk lace and other trimmings comprising a fashionable dress. An attempt was made to break the rigidity of the triangle into which woman had reduced her figure, although the method adopted—an enlargement of sleeves—had the effect of concealing the narrowness of the waist, and so intensifying the triangular effect.

Skirts were heavily flounced, and the favourite materials for ball dresses were tulle, crape, or tarlatan. Pearls, and other gems, were fashionable as trimming, being used to gather in festoons the flounces of the dress. The sleeves of a bodice of 1857 are described as terminating in bracelets of coral.

Sleeves, which were considered as articles of lingerie, were extremely elaborate, sometimes consisting of puffed muslin or tulle confined at the wrist with coloured ribbon, and enriched with five or six rows of Valenciennes lace.

Boys' dresses were more sensibly designed than formerly, but little girls were still burdened with a mass of frills and feathers borrowed from the fashions of their elders.

1850-1860

THE Paris Exhibition of 1855, which was visited in state by Queen Victoria, had the effect of confirming the dominance of French fashions and facilitating their entry into England, and in nothing was the influence of France more potent than in millinery fashions. Bonnets, which tended to be placed very far back on the head, showing the hair as far back as the crown, were small but elaborate, artificial flowers (usually roses) being the most usual decoration. For indoor wear white muslin caps were popular, worked with ribbon or embroidery, and for the country or for sunny days some curiously wide hats were designed, made of rice straw, with a deep tulle fringe depending from the brim all the way round.

For the dressing of the hair, as for the trimming of the rest of the costume, there was, particularly towards the end of the decade, a rage for pearls. Hair-nets to enclose what was called the "torsade" of hair at the back of the head, were composed of strings of pearls, and these nets were edged with pearl fringe, with tassels of pearl at the back and sides and a "cordon" of pearls passed between the bandeaux of hair in front. Two or three rows of gold chain were sometimes worn in the same fashion. Ribbon head-dresses of pink, blue, cerise, or the popular *bouton d'or* were worn at the theatre.

With evening-dress carved and inlaid fans of mother-of-pearl or ivory were fashionable. They could also be made of black or white crape, spangled with gold or silver ornaments in the Spanish style.

1860

IT was in the early 'sixties that the crinoline achieved its most astonishing proportions. Woman's form was reduced to an isosceles triangle, for even the narrowness of the waist was concealed by the width of sleeves or the amplitude of cloaks. The effect was completed by the smallness of the head-wear, with the hair confined in close-fitting bonnets tied with a bow under the chin. A pretty face was all that was needed to be irresistible, for every other portion of the female figure was most effectively concealed. In France, the hey-day of the Second Empire was a period of great luxury and ostentation. Ball dresses, especially, were costly and magnificent, and precious stones began to be worn in ever-increasing numbers. In England the influence of the Court was calculated to restrain rather than to encourage extravagance, and the death of the Prince Consort in 1861 threw a cloud over social functions, which lasted for many years. However, the reign of the crinoline was just as lasting in England as in France, and even the dresses of little girls revealed the influence of the prevailing fashion. Men's formal attire showed very little change.

1860-1865

THE " pork-pie " hat and the chignon are very characteristic of the early years of the decade.

The crinoline was sometimes worn in the street with a skirt raised several inches from the ground, revealing ankle-boots or miniature Hessians, a fashion much caricatured and exaggerated in the pages of *Punch*. The drawing-up process (if the skirts were not cut short) was effected by a machine called the *cage américain*, an improvement on the ordinary crinoline.

For men, the sack coat and hard round hat made their appearance at much the same time as the famous " Dundreary " whiskers. Nothing is perhaps so strange to the modern eye as the latter, and their universality makes the period seem more foreign than much more distant epochs. Male attire became even more sombre than before, for the fancy waistcoat disappeared, and was succeeded by one made of the same material as the coat. Trousers, however, remained strongly patterned.

Dresses, for out-of-doors, were in general simple in cut and dark in colour, but when they were drawn up by interior laces, they revealed brightly coloured underskirts. For evening dresses light velvets in such colours as rose, pale green, lilac, or turquoise were much admired. Light cloth coats could be worn over dark dresses, and the Empress Eugénie started a fashion for various shades of brown *foulard des Indes* trimmed with black velvet.

1865-1870

THERE was a pronounced change in the shape of the skirt about 1868. It ceased to be triangular, to become more bottle-shaped, and by the end of the decade was only full behind. It is possible that the origin of the bustle is to be sought in the practice of looping up the outer skirt. By 1868 the underskirt had, in some dresses, become the important one, the upper skirt being caught up almost to the hips by interior fastenings. These fastenings were usually higher at the side than at the back, and the general effect is not very different from that of the typical dress of the early 'seventies. The supposition is strengthened by the appearance of dresses in which the overskirt was not drawn up. The back of the skirt descends in a straight, sloping line from the waist to the ground. There is no trace of the protuberance which was afterwards to become so exaggerated.

Underskirts and overskirts were sometimes worn in contrasting colours, but more frequently in different shades of the same colour. Combinations of brown silk and bright blue taffeta, or of green, and green and black checked taffeta, were not uncommon. Taffeta, indeed, seemed to have replaced velvet as the most popular material.

1860-1870

IN the early 'sixties women's hair assumed the typical chignon form, with the back hair confined in a net bag which hung from the top of the head to below the nape of the neck. Even when no net was used the form of hair-dressing was very much the same, and what modifications were attempted were to be seen chiefly in evening toilettes.

In the late 'sixties the hair was dressed very flat on top, with a large bun, sometimes almost the size of the head, projecting straight back. Sometimes it was worn loose over the shoulders with very youthful effect, or else with two long curls hanging down behind, almost to the waist. The hat continued to be the smallest part of the head-dress, completely failing to cover what was still called the chignon, although its characteristic form had been abandoned. Sometimes the hair was dressed in a cascade of curls at the back of the head, echoing very closely in its complicated convolutions the shape of the back of the skirt with its incipient bustle.

Men were in general bearded, and if they shaved at all it was generally the upper lip that was left bare. Hair was worn much longer than would be thought correct to-day, and was frequently brushed forward to produce curls above the ears.

1870

THE crinoline, as we have seen, disappeared in the late 'sixties, and women's dresses assumed the bunched-up-behind appearance which they retained (with some important modifications) for twenty years. But it was not only the shape of dresses which was modified. The effect of the War of 1870–71 on France, and hence on the whole world of Fashion, was considerable. The luxury and ostentation of the Empire were felt to be out of place, and greater simplicity prevailed both in material and in ornamentation. The new mood did not last long, and accessories of the *toilette* assumed a new importance, in particular gloves, which were better made and more carefully chosen than they had ever been before. The discovery of Japanese art served to revive the interest in fans.

In men's dress a new informality was creeping in, marked by the growing success of the sack coat, the ancestor of our modern lounge suit. From having been something of an eccentricity it became very common, and but for the fact that trousers were of a different material from the coat and waistcoat, the male dress of about 1870 would seem more modern than many of the fashions that were to follow it.

1870-1875

THE corsage usually had the effect of a cavalryman's tunic, the skirts of the jacket projecting over the bustle. The draped appearance of the back of the skirt was universal, and skirts had a great many narrow flounces. Walking dresses touched the ground and some were even provided with a train. The cut of the dresses became very complicated, and a contemporary writer complains that whereas in former times an outmoded dress could still be used for something, in the 'seventies garments were composed of so many fragments of different materials that their only after-use was for the manufacture of patch-work quilts. It was the general custom to cut the dress out of two different materials, one patterned, one plain, and then to make one portion of the dress of the plain material trimmed with the patterned, and the rest of the patterned material trimmed with the plain. Check patterns were in great demand, and colours sometimes strident.

In the early 'seventies the mass of curls at the back of the head assumed, sometimes, monstrous proportions. The hair was also dressed higher at the back than it had been, with the result that the hat, which was still small, was pushed forward over the forehead.

1875-1880

ALREADY, by 1876, the bustle was much less pronounced, and that smoothness over the hips so characteristic of the early 'eighties had begun to make its appearance. Trimmings were elaborate, lace itself being used, not as formerly only at the edges of garments, but sewn onto their surface in *cascades*, *chutes*, or *ondulations*. There were shawls, fichus, and scarves in plenty, although a fashion writer of the period remarks that they were likely to be draped anywhere rather than round the neck.

Dresses tended to be comparatively simple in front and extremely complicated behind, with back fastenings (genuine or for ornament) of knots, bows, and even of fringed tassels.

A favourite material was "faye," either for evening or morning dresses, as it could be worked with embroidery or combined with figured velvet. Favourite colours were verdigris, blue marine, or pale blue, but the corsage was sometimes constructed, in deliberate contrast, of some such material as garnet velvet. Indian shawls were much used, worked up into the fashionable shapes of dolman or polonaise.

1870-1880

HATS, throughout the decade, tended to be very small, and perched high on the head. They were frequently made of felt, with extremely narrow brims and high crowns. To lift the hat still farther from the head the trimming was frequently placed underneath the front brim as well as on top. Little feather toques were worn for variety, as well as hats made entirely of ribbon. The bonnet had become so reduced in size as to be distinguished from the hat, if at all, only by the ribbon tied beneath the wearer's chin.

There is usually a consonance between the general form of dress and the form of coiffure. Hair, like clothes, tended to be drawn backwards, leaving the front of the head-dress comparatively simple and falling downwards at the back in a complicated arrangement of bands and twists reminiscent of the folds and flounces at the back of the skirt. This effect was enhanced by the fashion of weaving into the hair strands of ribbon or sprays of foliage. The face was left very free, and the ears were almost always visible.

1880

THE bustle may now be said to have disappeared, although it was to appear again later. However, although the bustle had gone, dresses were still looped up behind, but lower. The back of the dress still tended to be its most elaborate part. The figure was treated as a framework on which fringed draperies could be looped and crossed, much in the fashion of the heavy window curtains of the period. Waists were very narrow, and they accentuated the apparent rigidity of the form beneath its wrappings. An attempt was made to keep the top portion of the costume very sleek, following as closely as possible the lines of the corset, and then below the hips to flare out in frills, and bows, and trimmings.

Colours were violent, plum trimmed with electric blue, or royal blue with an edging of scarlet being not uncommon. Their garishness was, however, mitigated by the almost invariable custom of wearing white lace frills at the throat and wrists. Evening-gowns were, in general, not cut so low as they had been. Men's dress had assumed its modern hue and cut.

1880-1885

THE eclipse of the bustle was very brief. Indeed, it appeared in an exaggerated form fairly early in the new decade. There was a revival of interest in the Empire period, although so-called Empire dresses bore only the most shadowy resemblance to their prototypes. The simplicity of the Empire style was entirely lacking. Extremely complicated dresses were constructed of taffeta and tulle combined, three skirts of the latter being frequently superimposed on a "sheath-skirt" of the former, or a skirt of silk was decorated with three, five, or seven "volans" of pleated tulle.

Day gowns had a certain "tailor-made" effect, especially in the bodice, which lent itself to the use of somewhat heavy materials, of which wool was the chief constituent. Hats were, in general, small, and somewhat masculine in shape, and their decoration—feathers, ribbons, or artificial flowers—was discreet. The very small bonnet tied with broad ribbons under the chin was still fashionable. The hair was worn fairly close to the head.

1885-1890

DRESSES, in the second half of the decade, were somewhat shorter, although the bustle was as pronounced as it had ever been. Bodices were not quite so masculine in cut. They followed the lines of the figure very closely, but the hard line between bodice and skirt was, in general, less noticeable. The liking for woollen materials persisted, and there was a rage of Scottish plaid patterns even in Paris. For evening toilettes for very young women it was usual to have a corsage of satin and a skirt of gauze, generally of different colours. Those who did not desire to dance wore trains. *Décolletage* was not extreme. After being eclipsed for a time by the *décolleté en cœur*, the square opening came back into favour, although for those who were afraid of being thought too thin the round opening was preferred. White gloves were, of course, *de rigeur*, and precious stones, particularly diamonds, were worn in great numbers. Hats were still sometimes worn at the theatre, but were so small as to cause little inconvenience. Hats for the street were also extremely small, although the trimming was sometimes built up to a considerable height. Hair was dressed in a small bun on the very top of the head.

The straw hat for men became very popular, not only for boating, but the silk hat held its own for ordinary wear.

1880-1890

WOMEN'S hats in this decade were, in general, small, and hair-dressing comparatively simple. A kind of compromise was evolved between the hat and the bonnet with strings, and the result grew less and less like the latter, and more and more like the former. Plumes, artificial flowers, and a blend of the two became fashionable, and complete stuffed birds were sometimes used for the trimming of hats. The hat tended to rise more and more off the head as the decade progressed, and in 1890 the front brim, which was much larger than the rest of the hat, rose steeply above the forehead. The male straw hat and felt hat were adopted by women with sporting inclinations.

Men's headgear showed a new informality. The bowler hat and the fishing cap (with brim all round) made their appearance. Vests were buttoned very high, and very little linen was exposed to view. Whiskers were no longer worn, but the moustache was almost universal.

1890

IN England, costume is inevitably modified, from time to time, in the direction of informality, by the influence of country life. The male fashions of the early nineteenth century all over Europe were the direct outcome of the Englishman's passion for riding. These fashions had gradually been formalised, and the new enthusiasm for athletics at the end of the century led to the invention of the "Norfolk jacket" and the re-discovery of knickerbockers. The complete monopoly of trousers, which had lasted since the early years of the century, was over at last.

Women's walking dresses were still cumbrous enough, and still too tight-waisted, but even in feminine attire the influence of sport was beginning to make itself felt. About 1890 also began the passion for fine underclothes, which has lasted until our own day, and was perhaps originally provoked by the plainness of the fashionable tailor-made. It seemed an added refinement to allow luxuries of dress to be almost, if not entirely, concealed beneath a plain exterior. The manufacture of extremely fine materials received an immense impetus from the new demand.

1890-1895

ONE of the distinguishing marks of the early 'nineties was the revival of the wide sleeves of 1830. Indeed, Fashion has probably never so nearly repeated itself. The silhouette of 1830 and that of 1895 are almost identical, except that in the former the skirt was considerably shorter and the waist not so narrow. Some of the hats were surprisingly similar also, although the method of hair-dressing was different. The main difference in the sleeve was that in the 'nineties only the upper arm was puffed, giving rise to the famous "leg-of-mutton" appearance so typical of the period.

Skirts were long and trailing, but were comparatively simple in cut. The "wasp-waist" had assumed its most exaggerated and pernicious form. The bodice was close-fitting, and so great was the importance attached to sleeves that even in evening-dress small puffs of ribbon were sometimes attached to the shoulders to give the fashionable effect. In the street, muffs were almost universally carried, and were small, so that they could be carried on one forearm, the other hand being perpetually occupied in lifting the dress.

1895-1900

EVENING dresses, so long as the puffed sleeve was given its due importance, could be cut very low in front, but in general bodices were designed to fit closely round the neck, and occasionally a miniature Elizabethan ruffle was added behind. A considerable quantity of often costly lace was worn, at the wrists or in the form of a frilled shirt front attached to the corsage.

Capes were fashionable throughout the decade, and their forms, echoing those of the garments, were sometimes provided with raised shoulders.

The "Norfolk jacket" for men has been already mentioned. Cycling brought in knickerbockers for women, worn with over-tunics of mannish cut, and a very small hat. Children's dresses were more sensible than they had been for some time.

The most striking innovation during the last few years of the century was the blouse—thought to have been derived from the earlier "garibaldi," a shirt-like garment which, at first, was always red, like that of the Italian general from whom it took its name. The waist was still terribly constricted, but the wasp-like effect was diminished by allowing the bodice to hang over the now universal belt.

1890-1900

BLOUSES were popular, and their fronts could be very elaborate with heavy frills of Valenciennes -lace. Necks were high, and in evening-dress were sometimes encircled somewhat tightly by four or five rows of pearls or brilliants, a fashion now associated in most minds with Queen Alexandra.

About 1895 the most fashionable hat was a very small toque, to which Bird of Paradise plumes, arranged in a vertical aigrette in the centre, were an almost inevitable addition. Jet was much prized as a decoration for millinery, and it could be mingled with artificial flowers of much exaggerated size—mammoth violets or gigantic roses. Spotted veils were common, especially with the very small hats. Towards the end of the decade there was a growing tendency for hats to have wider brims and to be placed flat on the top of the head.

Men often wore a single collar, straight up all the way round, with (in evening-dress) a rather small and very flat white tie. Moustaches were still worn by almost every man, but beards had largely gone out of favour.

1900

THE end of the century is reached, but there is as yet no sign of the revolution which is to take place in women's clothes during the next twenty-five years. The corset was designed to throw the hips back and the bust forward in the most exaggerated manner possible. The lines of clothes followed those of the so-called *Art Nouveau*, with its swirling curves and its restless decorations. Even walking dresses had long trains collecting the dust of the streets at every step. The influence of sport had already produced costumes of varying degrees of usefulness, but that influence had not yet begun to affect fashionable attire.

For men of almost every position formal dress was still the usual costume, and the silk hat still reigned supreme. Indeed, the century as a whole exhibits far less striking modifications of costume than might have been expected from what was, in every respect, so revolutionary an epoch. Yet the clothes of the Nineteenth Century, viewed in retrospect, seem curiously appropriate. There is an intimate connection between costumes and manners, but no one knows exactly what it is.